AF413315

HOW TO GET INTO YOUR

Goldilocks Zone

5 Steps to Make the Best of Your Life on This Planet

ROHIT R. CHOWDHRY

notionpress.com

INDIA · SINGAPORE · MALAYSIA

Notion Press Media Pvt Ltd

No. 50, Chettiyar Agaram Main Road,
Vanagaram, Chennai, Tamil Nadu – 600 095

First Published by Notion Press 2021
Copyright © Rohit R. Chowdhry 2021
All Rights Reserved.

ISBN 978-1-63904-643-0

Advance Praise from the Field

How to get into your Goldilocks Zone

"I knew I wanted to be a dancer when I was five. What I didn't know was that one day I would become a Bharatanatyam dancer. I have promoted Indian dance and culture internationally throughout my life and today I aspire for greater accomplishments. Dance achieves its full beauty when there is an effervescence of emotion and expression in tune with the melody and rhythm. In the same way I believe your "*Goldilocks Zone*" is the perfect combination of elements that enables you to be the best version of yourself in your life. While destiny plays its part, **you need to do self-pondering and this could be at any point of time in your life.** Go for this book, **find your rhythm**, it's never too late."

– **Kumari Devayani,** International Bharatanatyam
Dance Performer & Choreographer, India; Recipient of the
Padma Shri Award 2009 in Bharatanatyam

"I am a fitness enthusiast, I love sports, and I was a tennis champ representing the state. I followed my passion of spreading happiness and fitness and making them accessible to various sections of society. Country Club was an outcome of my passion. I feel gratified that we are consistently contributing to support our communities through socially relevant programmes and events. I am glad that Rohit Chowdhry has come up with this book. He has focused on **pursuing your passion in alignment with your purpose and principles.** Our life is like our company, we own it. I encourage you to think like entrepreneurs and have a sound plan to implement what you want to accomplish. This book will help you in that. Go for it!"

– **Y. Rajeev Reddy,**
Founding Chairman & Managing Director
of Country Club (I) Ltd.

"This is indeed an excellent topic for the current times – particularly with the impact of Covid, work from home, less social and physical activity. The overall mental health is deteriorating all over the world. Step back and think through the 3 stages of our life – Learning, Earning and Giving. This book can make it easy in creating a purpose for our life. We all are striving for Peace and Happiness, which are about feeling good, proud, excited, satisfied and looking forward to tomorrow. This can only happen with **inner engineering**. Rohit has done an excellent job in simplifying this into 5 steps. I recommend this book to anyone who wants to make the best of their life, **bringing together their heart, mind and soul.**"

– **Sai Gundavelli,** Founder & CEO,
Solix Technologies Inc., California, USA
www.Solix.com

"People often take a long time to "get into their groove" because they need to find that sweet spot where they love their work, make a living, and yet it does not feel arduous – both **the journey as well as the destination thus becoming key.** This book by Rohit – who I have known for well over two decades for being very thoughtful while at the same time witty – makes this effort within reach. Action oriented with a fresh perspective, the book provides that essential push you need to change 'your orbit'. Pick it up!"

– **Srini Annamaraju,** CEO and Board Member,
21C Digital Holdings, London UK

"Insightful and timely. As our world becomes ever more rushed, using stories and well established theories, this book gives us **a means to understand our purpose** and navigate our way through life."

– **Bernard O'Brien,** Management Consultant,
Strategy, London, UK

"My journey from being a home maker to being crowned as a model involved a lot of planning, preparation and above all a lot of passion. It wasn't a bed of roses, as no journey is. I too fell and learnt a lot of important life lessons. I am also dedicated to community development works focusing on helping differently abled kids and creating awareness on health and fitness. *How to get into your Goldilocks Zone* is a book that will **help you to lead a life of satisfaction and content**. I appreciate that Rohit Chowdhry has supported his observations in this book with statistics from his research. I strongly recommend you to pick this book, as it will definitely help you in your journey of life!"

– Dr. Sudha Jain,
MS Asia Pacific 2017 (1st runner up),
Show coach & socialist, Hyderabad, India

"Many of us often end up doing something different from our passion in our career journey. In such a scenario sometimes, mid-life crisis hits earlier in life. This is an opportunity for one's self to **take stock, reshape and restart to explore one's true purpose and passion.** This book does just that; helps take the time in investing in one's self, and to make the best of one's life. Rohit has shared the five steps to embark on this journey, in a very effective way. I found the exercises to be very beneficial in self-discovery as you make progress through each of the steps. Try out the suggested tools; I am sure this will inspire you to build a purposeful and satisfying life."

– Rajat Raheja, Division President,
Amdocs India and Amdocs Cyprus, Pune, India

"The book offers unique insight, combining both **spiritual and corporate perspectives on progression and achieving one's goals.** The author shares personal experience to highlight practical steps that can be taken to direction in life using values and purpose to define a new path. Well written and structured it is accessible to all levels of professionals. The author has managed to produce something insightful that is very much 'of its time'."

– **David Gill,** International Head of Real Estate, AECOM, London, UK

"In the "Social Media" world, many seem to have aspirational values far exceeding the values of self-discipline, commitment and hard work. **Values and ethics continue to remain key differentiators amongst those creating a legacy.** The 5 steps to get into the "Goldilocks Zone" can prove to be the best mantra to make the best of one's life. My most favorite pick out of the five would be "principles". These truly define who you are. I believe this book is relevant as a map. This book hits all the most important aspects that are required to achieve a sense of accomplishment, satisfaction and contentment from a fulfilling career."

– **Raj Sivaraju,** Partner & President APAC, Arete IR, India; Founder of Sabrentkaro.com

"The ***Goldilocks zone* is a life plan**, a strategy for living your best life starting now. Rohit Chowdhry has taken the concept into an in-depth exploration of how it can work for each one of us. The worksheets and exercises have been particularly helpful and I recommend you **try answering some of the questions they raise**. You will surprise yourself."

— **Geeta Rao,** Writer, influencer,
Mumbai, India;
former Creative Director Ogilvy

"A lot of books talk about pursuing your passion and building skills. **While you put in the effort to discover your interests, it is equally critical to have a plan** that helps you understand what the challenges are, the hurdles you're likely to face and how you should mitigate these. This book emphasises on action, helping you develop and implement a strategy to accomplish your purpose and passion. Rohit has weaved in his wisdom and corporate experience very well in making sure rubber meets the road smoothly for you."

— **Fahad Samar,** Author of bestsellers,
Director at Bombay Talkie Films, Mumbai

"In this amazing book, Rohit tackles a question that vexes many of us: how to balance work and life, while finding meaning and purpose in both. As a mentor to so many talented professionals over the course of his career, Rohit now shares his wisdom to help you understand how to channel your God-given talents into a vocation that is fulfilling emotionally, intellectually and spiritually. The *"Goldilocks"* concept is so appropriate here, as you **forge a career path that is both challenging and rewarding over time, without extinguishing the flames of your passion or flying too close to the sun.**"

— **Stuart Sechriest,** Marketing Director,
Cognizant Technology Solutions, Miami, Florida, USA

"Rohit blends seasoned experience and sensitive coaching to his debut work. In all the years, I have known him, his emotional intelligence had shone through his work. Now he distils his insights into a set of practical tools that anyone can apply to his life. In fact, Rohit extends himself by forcing questions beyond work or success. **Life's perennial questions need to be answered around purpose and then measure one's success in the context of fulfilment.** The world of *Goldilocks* is a wonderful metaphor for people to latch on to the notion that success cannot be divorced from larger ideals one espouses. Well done Rohit and I wish you expansive success for this book."

– **Sunil Robert Vuppula,** Leadership Coach and Author, India; Follow on twitter#sunilrobert www.sunilrobert.com

"Finding one's true calling in life is like taking the great leap of faith. It calls for a lot of courage to press the Pause button, and getting off the treadmill of the run-of-the-mill existence that we have become accustomed to, but are not really comfortable with. I discovered my true calling as a writer when I was 55, having spent more than 25 years as a techy. **If Rohit's book was around earlier I am sure it would have nudged me into my true calling much earlier.** His book provides the compass to successfully navigate and find the proverbial pot of gold at the end of the rainbow."

– **Srinivasa Raghavan Narayanan,** Partner, Metaplexity Associates, India; Author of books – Amma and Miracle

"The world we live in today is busy and noisy and becoming more so every day. Humans, me included, often struggle balancing what we need to do and what we want to do while also being mindful of our mental wellbeing. It's hard work and can be exhausting. Wisdom and experience certainly make finding that balance easier. But what if we had the tools and coaching available to find that balance earlier in life? *How to get into your Goldilocks Zone* **delivers those tools and coaching through simple and straightforward principles that can be applied immediately to one's life**. Finding that balance is still hard work, but this book makes it easier and can help you find your life balance sooner."

– **Steve Schmith,** Executive Director,
Automotive News, St. Louis, Missouri, USA

"Strategic read. I have known Rohit for decades now. He is very creative in his thought process with an eye on the overall strategy, always. This book is for folks who have started to work and are now seeking to channelise their work lives into a meaningful career. This book **helps you move to a zone closer to what you would want to do, which in turn will help you make the best of your life.** The book shares an interesting 5 point framework to get into your *Goldilocks Zone* and has interesting self-assessment exercises which lead to a personalized action plan. I highly recommend this book, it is time well invested!"

– **Gurmit Singh,** (former CEO of Forbes India,
former Managing Director of Yahoo)
Currently with Quora, the world's best
known knowledge sharing site/App

* * * * *

This book is dedicated to my family, friends, colleagues, clients, stakeholders, teachers, mentors and coaches, all of whom have left an impact on a lot that has gone into this book.

Contents

Foreword by Dr. Annurag Batra

From the first time I met Rohit Chowdhry several years ago in Hyderabad on a business trip, I knew he always wanted to do something that would help people. I recollect the meeting in which he proposed a tie-up with my organisation to offer customized hiring solutions for a specific market segment. I am more than happy to write this foreword for Rohit's book "How to get into your Goldilocks Zone".

Just over twenty-three years ago, with a cup of tea, I was reading this premier business magazine – BW | Businessworld, and today it is my cup of tea. In 2013 we acquired BW | Businessworld. Dreams really do come true! I learnt that life is always full of surprises! Twists, turns and new opportunities. Rohit's book focuses on how do you lead a life that is purposeful and at the same time in tune with your abilities and capabilities. It helps you find answers to such questions and in turn helps you make the best of your life.

I want to give back to the industry and my love for teaching comes into play in the advisory positions I hold. I regularly speak in national and international conferences on media, internet, television, media policy and entrepreneurship. I mentor budding entrepreneurs and I enjoy the process of reverse mentoring too as I learn from these young entrepreneurs. At BW Businessworld, BW Accelerate is an initiative to provide a structured platform to entrepreneurs for mentorship and growth. I have mentored several leaders, helping them discover their passion and have supported them to pursue their passion in a planned manner. I find similarities in how Rohit has emphasised in this book about the "strategy" which is a critical component that finally gets you to "do" what you aspire. I believe that if you make your hobby your profession, you don't have to work and life will be a blessing.

Rohit has an illustrious corporate career spanning 30 years, working with global stakeholders in MNCs. He is an expert in his field, advising leaders in setting up shared services, becoming more efficient, and helping grow the business. Building various teams and organisations, he has hired, trained, mentored and coached several management professionals. He is a certified coach and understands the hurdles people face in being successful at their careers and in being satisfied with their lives. Rohit is also an artist who expresses himself creatively around Indian culture. You can see his paintings in this book.

We as individuals are in search of meaning and more than ever live in a purposeful economy where each one of us is trying to find his or her Ikigai. Rohit as a transformation catalyst seems to have found his true purpose of life where all his areas of passion culminate – business consultant, mentor, coach, facilitator, artist – in engaging with people to support them to explore their full potential in living a satisfying life. Rohit deserves kudos for finding his own Goldilocks zone. Balance and Nirvana can co-exist is what I have learnt by reading this book.

This book is like a friend, like a coach, like a co-passenger who is guiding you, asking you the right questions in your journey of finding the purpose of your life, finding a profession or finding a gig. The story telling and the probing questions will get you to a point where you can get onto a journey of personal growth.

Personal Growth is never easy and I can say it first-hand. This book becomes your Personal Growth Assistant. The Goldilocks zone is Nirvana, its' pure bliss and this maiden book from Rohit is your pass to your dreams – both expressed and subliminal. We know what we do not know but sometimes we do not even know what we do not know. This book helps you discover your hidden talents and the direction you must take in life.

Rohit seems to have cracked the code by asking the right questions and leading one to the right answers. The answers are all within us but you need a guide, a coach, a facilitator. Rohit in his maiden book has poured his heart, his skill, his science, his art, his findings, his intuition in bringing the code to life. Based on his experiences and discovery journey, Rohit has developed and shared tools in this book that you could use to your benefit.

Capitalising from his experiences, he seems to have made it a purpose for himself to help people realise "their purpose" earlier in their lives so that they may benefit from leveraging the outcomes for the larger part.

If Covid has taught us one thing, it is the value of human life. We have finite time on earth and we have to make the best of our life and time on this planet. We have been given this gift of life and our unique talents and unique opportunities to curate a life which feels good on the inside and outside. The true purpose of life is a life of purpose. Life post Covid is driven by the three Cs – Compassion, Collaboration and Contactlessness.

My advice to you is that you cannot change your past but you can take a step back, plan well for your future, and implement the plan. This book helps you do that.

This book is a must for young professionals starting out, budding entrepreneurs, I would say CXOs who wish to get to a place "where their hobby becomes their profession and they are having fun and excelling." This book and the time you have invested in the book will help you make an impact – create a life of purpose. Now that you have bought this book, are reading it, read it at least twice.

May you find your Goldilocks zone.

— Dr. Annurag Batra, Entrepreneur, Author, Angel investor, TV show host. (Founder and Editor in Chief of exchange4media, managing several big names under its aegis. Chairman and Editor in Chief of BW Businessworld Media Group, one of the most respected business publications in the country. Member of the Board of Governors of the prestigious Management Development Institute, Gurgaon.)

* * * * *

Preface

The birds began to chirp. Far away the sun was slowly rising. The first crack of dawn was starting to turn the dark sky into a combination of golden yellow, orange and red. The sun was slowly radiating its warm glow on the window of my bedroom. The world was waking up but I had been lying awake for hours in my bed. This was my third consecutive sleepless night.

I went through this phase of restlessness a few years ago. My life seemed like it was going quite well, doing fine on the work front, home front, with day-to-day challenges, operational issues, but otherwise, going smoothly. One night I woke up with a lot of questions in my mind, and I was not very sure if I had the right answers to any of them. In the next few weeks my mind was working on a double shift, taking care of all the day stuff and trying to mull over the questions at night.

I felt like I was standing in a bookstore and asking for someone to guide me to the self-help section. There was no magical solution.

* * *

It took me a few months to find the resources and tools to get the answers to my questions. It was a journey of talking to my coaches, mentors, family members, colleagues, friends, relatives, my stakeholders, clients, reading a lot of articles on the internet, listening to TED talks and reading self-help books. While I thought I knew what I wanted to do in life, I had no idea what the purpose of my life was. This journey was the best investment of my time in self-discovery.

Each one of us wants to lead a happy life. A life that is satisfying. We want to be known for the contributions we have made. How good we have been as a child, as a parent, as an employee, or as an entrepreneur, a leader, a global citizen. We want our life to matter to others. We want to be known well after we are gone. We want to leave a positive personal legacy behind.

The question is – is everyone able to do this? Why is it that some leave behind a legacy, while others are just remembered? How do you lead a life that is purposeful and at the same time in tune with your abilities and capabilities?

Dear Reader, this book "How to get into the Goldilocks Zone" helps you find answers to these questions, and in turn helps you make the best of your life.

Why should you listen to me?

In my thirty years of working in corporate organizations, I have interacted with innumerable talented people, and have observed them closely: how a lot of people go to work each day to do what has been assigned to them to the best of their ability, and some others who are proactively reaching out to perform activities that they are passionate about. The latter are people who are living their dream – making each day satisfying and fulfilling. These are people who are not just waiting for the weekend, do not have Monday blues and are not just working to pay their bills.

I am a Certified Life Coach, a Certified Executive Coach, and a Certified Career Transition Coach, all by the International Coach Federation (ICF). I have coached and mentored many management level professionals, and hence understand the hurdles people face in being successful at their careers and in being satisfied with their lives. Some of the key themes of the conversations have been around leveraging one's strengths, identifying one's passion, behavioral changes, relationship building, remaining calm in a crisis, strategic mindset, possibilities for introverts and career transition.

I stumbled on this path of self-discovery rather late in life, in fact, my early forties. I would really like to help my fellow beings go through this process earlier in their lives so that they may benefit from leveraging the outcomes for the larger part. The earlier one starts on this journey knowing what they would like it to be, the more fulfilling that journey will be. We potentially limit making the best of our life by not discovering our purpose, and not because of any limitation related to our abilities, capabilities, skills and competencies. Life becomes more focused, motivating and meaningful if we have identified the purpose.

In this book, I have shared my learning from that journey. Understand how to find your purpose and passion, use it to leverage your skills and capabilities, and develop and implement a strategy to move forward. Based on what I learnt, I have also developed a few tools that you could use to your benefit. These inputs will help you save the physical struggle of searching for stuff or talking to several people or professionals. Nevertheless, it certainly requires you to invest mentally, to go through a unique journey of self-discovery. This book will help you not only to explore the purpose of life but also take the next step of identifying a strategy to fulfill that purpose. It would be apt to say that leading a life of purpose is also the purpose of life.

This journey is about moving from just making a living to making the best of life, not just having happy moments but instead, experiencing sustained satisfaction!

– Rohit R Chowdhry, Author

* * * * *

Acknowledgements

I take this opportunity to thank all those who have helped me during the process of writing this book.

Geeta Rao, Uma Shanker, Vandana Waghray, Rajeev Chowdhry, Aasheesh Chowdhry and Santosh GL for their valuable ideas and suggestions.

Srinivas Raghavan, Sukesh Koka and Jatin Gupta for their guidance to me as a first-time author.

My family and friends for their support with the research and survey.

All those who provided their valuable inputs and advance praise for the book.

Preeti my wife, for her support all through the journey of conceptualizing and getting this book to a final shape.

The Publishers Notion Press and their team for all their support in getting this book to you.

* * * * *

Chapter 1

What is the "Goldilocks Zone"?

"Ohhh, this porridge is too hot!" Goldilocks exclaimed.

Hungrily, she tasted the porridge from the second bowl. "This porridge is too cold."

She then tasted the last bowl of porridge. "Aaah, this porridge is just right!" she said happily. And she ate it all up.

* * *

Dear Reader, the Goldilocks principle is drawn from an analogy to the children's story "Goldilocks and the Three Bears", in which a little girl named Goldilocks tastes three different bowls of porridge and finds that she prefers porridge that is neither too hot nor too cold but has just the right temperature.

Astronomers have been inspired by this story and have applied this concept of the "right amount", coining the term "Goldilocks Zone". Astronomy has always had a significant impact on our universal view. Our ancestors identified and tracked the positions of the sun, moon and celestial bodies to develop calendars; they used this knowledge to decide when to plant crops, to predict weather and to navigate ships. Astronomy helps us in navigation even today, via GPS. Many technologies originally developed for astronomy are today being used for common applications close to our lives. It has also influenced peoples' creativity in writing books, making web series and sci-fi movies.

For many years, astronomers looked around the solar system. Mercury and Venus were too hot. Mars and the farther planets were too cold. Only the earth was just right for life. Our planet has a perfect combination of liquid water, a breathable atmosphere and a suitable amount of sunshine. That is a perfect combination of conditions.

If the earth were a little closer to the sun it might be too hot like Venus, a little farther and too cold like Mars. Somehow though, we ended up in just the right place with just the right ingredients for life to flourish. Researchers said we were in the "Goldilocks Zone".

The Goldilocks Zone refers to the habitable zone around a star where the warmth is just right – not too hot and not too cold – for water to exist on a planet.

As we know, water is essential for life and where we find water on earth, we also find life. Evidently, our earth is in the Goldilocks Zone around the sun. If earth were where the planet Pluto is, all its water would freeze; on the other hand, if the earth were where Mercury is, all its water would evaporate.

Each one of us is unique. We bring this individual perspective and value to the world based on our experiences, upbringing and way of thinking. Our passions differ; our strengths and capabilities differ. Therefore, the Goldilocks Zone for each one of us, to make the best of our lives, is distinctive. This zone is exclusive to you, depending on what you want to do, how you want to do it and why you want to do it.

Astronomy makes us conscious of how small we are, but how impactful we could be when we operate in our Goldilocks Zone, and how we fit into this vast scheme of things in the universe.

Your *Goldilocks Zone is the perfect combination of conditions where **you** can make the best of **your** life.*

In the next chapter you will know more about why you should get into your Goldilocks Zone, why this book is for you to read and what my survey data says.

*   *   *   *   *

Chapter 2

Why Get Into Your Goldilocks Zone?

As a kid I admired the telescope my older cousin had and I used to watch her look through the telescope at the sky. Her passion was astrophysics. After completing her engineering from IIT she left for the US for advanced studies. It was a moment of joy, an unforgettable memory, when she handed over the telescope to me. I remember watching the various star formations and being mesmerized by the sky.

My childhood ambition was to become a pilot. Watching planes fly across the blue sky captured my imagination. The speed, the sound, the high altitude, and sometimes the white streak of a withering cloud across the sky in their wake. Everything was fascinating.

At the age of ten I wanted to join the armed forces, specifically the air force. I joined a school that prepares students to lead as officers in the defence services. At the end of schooling, and after a few unsuccessful attempts to join the forces, I returned to being a fulltime civilian. I enrolled for a graduation in commerce in anticipation of becoming a chartered accountant. This was a complete shift from my original ambition.

During the break, between the commerce graduation exams and taking up the CA articleship, I decided to do a part-time computer awareness course in the evenings. This was way back in 1990 when computers were visible largely at airline booking offices or railway reservation counters.

One day at the training center, I saw a notice inviting summer trainees for marketing. The job was to scan the market for business opportunities to develop customized software applications and impart computer training. As I was free during the day time, I opted for this summer job. This led me to develop an interest in information technology as well as business development.

That was a start in building a thirty-year career in the IT industry and subsequently in IT enabled off-shore operations.

* * *

When we are young, we tend to be very clear in what we want to do. As we grow, we choose specific subjects and pursue our studies expecting to follow a straightforward path towards our desired career. Some people obsessively pursue a certain path because they know exactly what they want to do. Others may end up in a particular career quite by accident.

Sometimes the interview that you did best at on campus may land you your first job rather than the interview for which you prepared the most. You end up doing things you are told to do, provided feedback on, liking some of it and hating some. You see early promotions as an acknowledgement and encouragement of being on the right track, making lateral moves within the organization, to an area of interest, and sometimes changing to a new one.

To summarise, there are huge gaps between what people want to do versus what they end up doing. After spending a lot of time and energy, through trial and error, they tend to move to what they want to do.

The earlier you get into your 'Goldilocks Zone' the better. When you operate in your Goldilocks Zone, you will be actively creating the perfect combination of conditions to make the best of your life.

This book is for you to read if you...

- Have completed your basic education – like a Bachelors' or Masters' degree and taken up a job/ work assignment.

- Have worked in a job for a few years (you have an idea of what you like and what you do not).

- You feel restlessness and see something missing in your life.

- You are not sure if you are on the right career path.

- You are trying to understand yourself better by pursuing more meaning and fulfillment in life.

- You are trying to carve out a long-term path for yourself.

- You are waking up in the middle of the night wondering if your life is just stuck in a routine, run by mobile alarms and an electronic calendar.

If five or more of the above statements apply to you then you should read this book.

This is the time to take a step back from the noise in your life, to reinvent a new version of yourself – become more self-aware and lead your life more meaningfully.

You should read this book if you would like to know how to get into your 'Goldilocks Zone'. This book also provides tools for you to change what you are doing, how you are doing it, and more importantly, why you are doing it.

When our mind thinks of taking a step in a new logical direction, our heart wants to hold on to old ways. In such situations we need to delve deeper as to why our heart is holding us back and why we are uncomfortable taking the step. I truly believe that it is better to embark on this journey of self-discovery to make the best of your life than to be afraid that you may not get grand results and hence not embark on this journey.

The desire to find one's calling and to act upon it spans across age and salary groups.

Are these questions keeping you awake at night?

- What is my calling?

- What am I passionate about?

- How do I do what I want to do?

- What is the purpose of my life?

- Why am I doing what I am doing?

- How do I find satisfaction in my life?

- Why am I confused about who I am and where I am going?

- How do I get to be at peace with myself?

- How do I earn my living by doing what I like doing?

- How do I get up every morning energised and motivated?

All these questions are interwoven. To address and resolve these questions I believe you should be operating in your 'Goldilocks Zone'.

Which state describes you the best?

- You are dissatisfied with your life and are looking for motivation.

- You are superficially happy with your life and are looking for a strong reason to make the best of it.

- You are unable to find answers to your questions and are looking to discover them.

I have been through the phase of being superficially happy with my life and then rummaged around for a strong rationale to make the best of it. In retrospect, it was a very fulfilling phase of finding answers to my questions.

You can do yourself a great favour by bringing positive changes into your life. These changes begin by creating the conditions that allow you to listen to the voice of your calling. You then need to align your potential to this calling and take conscious steps in that direction.

It is important to note that getting into your 'Goldilocks Zone' is certainly possible and achievable for you. This book is built on practical steps to help you make the journey manageable and keep you motivated as you progress with each step of the journey.

You are not alone. Outcomes of my survey:

As I started to write this book, I was keen to find out how others were doing with these questions. I ran an online survey in 2020 that had 565 respondents. I have provided an overview of the survey in the last chapter.

In summary, the respondents included those who had at least completed their Graduation in studies, a good gender mix, spread across age-groups, a mix of occupations and a combination of personality styles. Most of the respondents were in the age group of 36 – 55 (71%).

I have leveraged the survey results and have shared my observations and interpretations at appropriate junctures in the book. This will help you see the reasons behind what I am proposing more realistically.

Here are a few highlights for you upfront:

The quest for a purposeful life drives satisfaction in life.

According to my research, the quest for a purposeful life drives satisfaction in life for many respondents. Those who had discovered their purpose of life were 81% satisfied with their life, in comparison to 67% satisfaction for those who had not.

People need to invest their time and energy towards exploring their "purpose of life".

Based on the survey data, I inferred that people need to invest their time and energy towards exploring their "purpose of life". They seem to find this a bit abstract, as they seem to relate more with what they are "passionate" about.

The earlier one discovers their life's purpose, the more satisfied life they will lead.

Based on the research, this variance between the two segments is not as big as I would have expected it to be. The satisfaction percentage of those who had discovered their purpose of life before the age of 30 was 80%, while those who had discovered their purpose of life after 30 was 83%. As mentioned earlier, those who had not discovered their purpose of life had an average satisfaction of 67%, which is much lower than those who had discovered their life's purpose.

This also means that there's a stronger need for people to invest their time and energy towards exploring their "purpose of life". This is all the more reason for this book.

We wish we could just pay money to someone who could tell us how we could make our life meaningful.

99% of the respondents chose to invest an average of 43% of their annual earnings to make their life meaningful.

Considering the average salary of an Indian MBA to be about Rs. 677,000 (Source: Glassdoor, Jan'21); this investment would be at least Rs. 290,000. I am not claiming that my advice in this book is worth (just) Rs. 290,000, but I certainly believe that if you implement all the steps, then it would certainly be worth much more than that in terms of the satisfaction with your life.

Sometimes people are entangled in jobs or work because of their early choices in life. While it may take long, it is never too late to make a course correction.

People experience a midlife psychological low.

According to my research, the rating on satisfaction in life, generally has an up-curve in a person's life. There is a steep rise between the ages of 31–40 but there is a visible dip in the age group of 41–50 before it starts to improve.

Midlife crisis is brought about by events that are emphasized by a person's growing age, imminent mortality and possible dissatisfaction with accomplishments in life. Nowadays this crisis is happening earlier in life. As our wake-up calls get younger, the need to understand the reasons and take actions becomes paramount.

Move ahead. The next chapter is about how to get into *your* Goldilocks Zone.

* * * * *

Chapter 3

How to Get Into Your Goldilocks Zone?

Once upon a time, there was a person called Wolsam, who finished his studies and was working in a place called Nylkoorb. He was paid well, his job was stable, and he lived a comfortable life. But there was a feeling of loneliness and so he began looking for a life partner.

That year, during the festive season, he found his love Ahtreb, and they got married. They lived happily and had two children. Their schedules became predictable around their work, children, family, friends, celebrations, outings etc. One weekend Wolsam and Ahtreb talked about the discontent in their lives. They decided to set aside time to plan and execute something they really wanted to accomplish in life. As they discussed, planned and implemented actions they experienced a sense of accomplishment and felt happy about it. Their work was getting recognized and they were felicitated with awards. Their children Nella and Nna started getting busy with their higher studies and careers.

While Wolsam and Ahtreb were in general happy with their life, they felt the need to give back to the society. They had a series of discussions over this, and decided to start a non-profit organization that catered to a certain need of the neighbourhood. Spending time with the needy and supporting the community gave them immense satisfaction. They were now at peace with themselves and the way their lives had shaped up.

* * *

Dear Reader, now that you know what the Goldilocks Zone is, let us look at how you can get into this zone.

Topics covered in this chapter:

- Abraham Maslow's 'hierarchy of needs'

- Moving onward and upward

- Why I think that being in the Goldilocks Zone will help you make the best of your life

- Overview of the 5 steps for you to get into your Goldilocks Zone

In the story you just read, I have reflected on the different hierarchy of needs as per Maslow. The names of people and places used in the story are 'suoititcif' ('fictitious' spelled backwards, along with other names like Maslow, Bertha, Brooklyn etc.). In his 1943 paper "A Theory of Human Motivation", Abraham Maslow proposed the 'hierarchy of needs'. Maslow used the terms 'physiological', 'safety', 'belonging and love', 'esteem', and 'self-actualization' to describe the pattern through which human motivation generally moves. This means that each of these stages contains certain needs that must be met in order for an individual to complete their hierarchy, and attain the 'self-actualization' stage. His theory is based on the assumption that the lower needs must be satisfied before a person can achieve their potential and self-actualize, which may not always be the case.

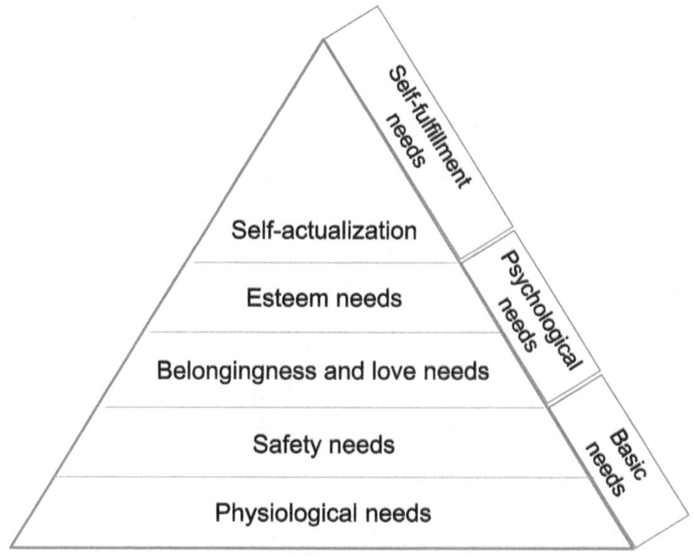

You must have faced it practically in life so far as well. To live we first need the basics – food, clothing and shelter. If a person has no regular source of food or does not have a place to stay, they may not be concerned about their calling, rather be worried about their next meal.

At the start of your career, you would have been more interested in securing your job by working hard, delivering what is expected of you, constantly learning – up-skilling/re-skilling and going beyond expectations. As you become more stable in your job and career, you look for a partner, someone with whom you can share an intimate bond, share your emotions, deep feelings, concerns, inhibitions, desires and aspirations.

When you have a family, you look forward to the love of your children.

On the work side, with the value you deliver, you get promotions, titles, recognition, awards etc. By this time, you have already worked for ten to fifteen years. As you work harder and deliver more value to your organization, you keep getting accolades, fancier titles, hikes, bigger bonuses, more perks. You set high benchmarks for others and also improve your standard of living. You end up buying a bigger house, more expensive/branded stuff, fancy gadgets, flashy cars, send your children to bigger/better institutions for study.

Is life about fulfilling needs? How long does this phase last? What's next after this? Is retirement the next step? What do you do after retirement?

If you are unable to answer these questions you're not alone.

In a study from 2011, researchers from the University of Illinois examined the association between need fulfillment and subjective well-being across 123 countries. While they found that many of the needs Maslow described appeared to be universal, the order in which these needs are met had little impact on people's satisfaction with life. This implies that higher-level needs like feeling respected, social support and autonomy were paramount even though the lower-level needs were not being fulfilled.

At the self-actualization phase, one looks for self-fulfillment. Unlike the previous phase, you are not competing with anyone, it is all about what you really want to accomplish, and what standards you are going to set for yourself. In this phase you are not trying to improve your capabilities, rather you are making the best of your strengths to do what you really want to do.

Moving onward and upward

Maslow's model is usually represented in the structure of a pyramid, but it doesn't need to be visualized like that.

Imagine moving up the hierarchy based on your changing perspectives of life and your needs. At each stage, you are constantly orbiting around your role based on your passion, strengths and capabilities.

Imagine you are a planet revolving around the Sun, (which is your job role/work) which you do based on your interests, capabilities and aspirations. You are constantly spinning on your axis to do your day-to-day stuff. You have your stakeholders who interact closely with you, like the moon revolving around you. Imagine now that you want to move to a different vertical orbit, that attracts you not necessarily for a higher monetary reward, but instead takes you closer to your passion and allows you to use your strengths and capabilities more effectively and makes you happier and more content. The Goldilocks Zone – is a term I am using to describe a state in which you enjoy yourself the most and are thriving, and are able to make the most of your life.

Why do I think that being in your Goldilocks Zone will help you make the best of your life?

When you face a problem, you are worried and feel disturbed. You then sit back and think about the various solutions, evaluate them, identify the best one, and start implementing it. Once you start implementing the solution, the problem is no more a worry for you.

A lot of people live their lives having no clue what they want to ultimately accomplish, usually following the expectations and dreams of others – parents, peers, friends, children, even neighbours!

Ultimately, we all want to be happy, contented and lead a meaningful life, don't we? The answer is in understanding our long-term objective, identifying the path towards it and start progressing on that path. This will help us to be at peace with ourselves.

We also have the responsibility towards ourselves to make our life worthwhile with our unique purpose.

Happiness and contentment are accomplished not through worldly/materialistic aspects but by accomplishing the higher objective or purpose of life. Once the purpose of life is clear, it becomes a lot easier to identify the path to it. Keeping this in mind, I have come up with the following steps for you to get into your Goldilocks Zone:

- Understand the WHY: Understand your PURPOSE of life.

- Identify the WHAT and HOW:

  o   What is your PASSION?

  o   What are your key SKILLS?

> o   How do you go about accomplishing your
>   passion? What is your STRATEGY?
>
> •   All through this journey, keep in view your way of
>   life; your character, your individual way of dealing
>   with day-to-day situations. All these are your
>   framework or PRINCIPLES.

I will address these key steps in the following sequence:

- Principles – the overarching framework

- Purpose – answers the WHY

- Passion & Skills – answers the WHAT

- Strategy – answers the HOW

Below is a pictorial representation of the P^3S^2 model for you to move into your Goldilocks Zone. Each of the elements is in harmony with the other.

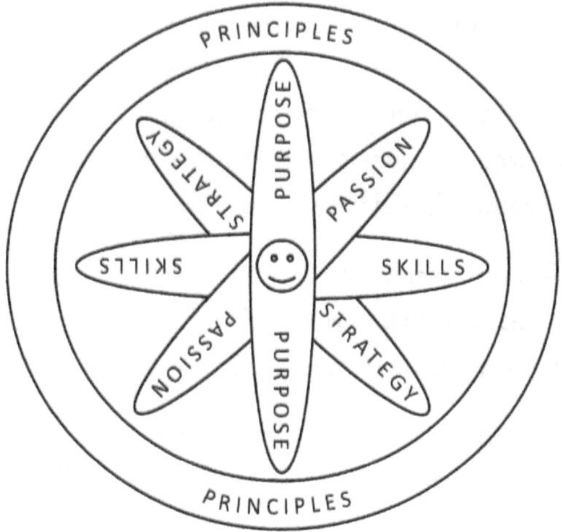

To reach your identified PURPOSE, you need to identify your PASSION and SKILLS, develop and implement a STRATEGY, all the while abiding by PRINCIPLES.

> When people are able to see their purpose clearly and make progress on it, they distinguish themselves in the following manner:
>
> - Appreciate authenticity and uncertainty
>
> - Remain focused, objective, creative, community oriented, down to earth, not worried about having a different opinion, open to possibilities, realistic.
>
> - Have clarity of thought, a strong human connection, a high moral standard
>
> - Feel connected to nature, feel a sense of gratitude

When I think of legendary personalities who had clarity of purpose, identified their passion and skills, developed and implemented a strategy, while abiding by their principles – the following come to mind – Mahatma Gandhi, Martin Luther King Jr., Nelson Mandela, Mother Teresa. A few more who have been recognized for their contribution with the Nobel prize – Wangarĩ Maathai, Malala Yousafzai, Muhammad Yunus.

While these famous personalities have been recognized globally for their contributions, if you look more closely, you will find role models in your own community and network.

These are people like you and me who *made choices around what they would like to do for the benefit of the community, have gone above & beyond expectations, and have responded to challenges (that many face) in an extraordinary manner.*

Here are a few from recent times, that I find very inspiring:

- Indian industrialists known for their business ethics and philanthropy – Ratan Tata, Azim Premji.

- Those who have fought back circumstances – Gauri Sawant (towards recognition of transgender as the third gender), Laxmi Agarwal (an acid attack survivor, towards regulating the sale of acid).

- Contributors towards right to information and education – Aruna Roy (right to information), Kailash Satyarthi (campaigned against child labour and advocated the universal right to education), Shaheen Mistry (after-school tutoring to children from low-income communities).

- Environmentalists – Jadav "Molai" Payeng (over four decades has planted and tended trees on a sandbar of the river Brahmaputra, turning it into a forest reserve of about 1,360 acres), Latika Nath (a wildlife conservationist).

- Personalities who have leveraged their popularity and fame for social causes – Sachin Tendulkar, Mary Kom, Sonu Sood.

Dear Reader, take a pause here and think of your own family, extended family, relatives, colleagues and friends who had clarity of purpose, identified their passion and skills, developed and implemented a strategy, while abiding by their principles.

Overview of the 5 steps for you to get into your Goldilocks Zone

In the subsequent five chapters, I shall elaborate on each of the five steps that help you get into your Goldilocks Zone. Before you move to the next chapter, let me briefly explain through the following table, how these steps are different from each other and yet obviously related.

Principles
• A framework to look back on when faced with a dilemma.
• A path of self-discipline.
• Helps you be a role-model. Helps you lead the path of righteousness.

Purpose	
• Answers the 'Why'.	• It is the legacy you want to leave.
• It is your motivation to do what you do.	• You may be able to see your Purpose by connecting the dots of your life experiences.
• Purpose needs to be built.	
• You live your own life (not as defined by others or as an obligation). Purpose helps you become who you were meant to be. It stems from your authentic self.	• Purpose involves serving others.
	• Purpose is focused.
	• Forms the foundation for your Passion.

Passion	**Skills**
• Answers the 'What'. • Your compelling emotions behind your dreams. • Things that you do most often by choice. • Starting on your Passion takes you closer to your Purpose. • Passion can be found. • You can be passionate about multiple aspects in life and be prepared to make sacrifices for them.	• Answers the 'What'. • Your unique qualities: those that come naturally to you. • Aspects that you are good at that have always fetched compliments.

Strategy
• Answers the 'How'. • The overarching method or path chosen for achieving the objectives, including specific plans.

As you proceed, I would like to call out a couple of aspects.

- First, each chapter ends with a section called 'In a nutshell' where I have captured the key messages of the chapter.

- Second, each chapter also includes certain 'exercises' with space for you to take notes in response to those exercises. I would strongly urge you to make your notes in the space to avoid having to refer to another document.

In the next chapter you will read about Principles – the first step to be in your Goldilocks Zone.

* * * * *

My acrylic painting of a sunflower — always facing sunshine. Reminds us of the beauty and principles of nature.

To view the colour version scan this QR code.

Chapter 4

Step 1 – Principles

One Saturday afternoon I was picking up my son from school. He was about eight years old, in fourth standard. On our way back home, I had to hand over some documents to a chartered accountant who had his office in a narrow lane. I stopped near his office, let my son stay in the car and went up to give the documents, hoping to return in a couple minutes.

When I returned to the car, my son was sobbing. On enquiring, he told me that a large van was trying to go past our car in the lane and that the van driver found it very difficult to maneuver as our car was blocking the path. The driver and a few others in the van kept abusing the car owner (me) as they struggled and went past. My son was very disturbed with this episode. I apologized to my son for the situation I had placed him in. As we returned home, I also apologized for not parking the car in the right place.

As I reflected on the situation, I also thought about the sort of example I was setting for my son, and why did I not take a few extra minutes to park the car at a proper parking slot than take a short-cut.

* * *

To be in your Goldilocks Zone, one of the foremost aspects is to do the right thing, adhere to Principles. Let's explore more about Principles in this chapter.

Principles, in the context of this book, provide us with a frame of reference to look back upon, when we have a dilemma. It is a path of self-discipline.

Topics covered in this chapter:

- Categorizing Principles

- How to be ethical?

- Your Ethics Quotient Assessment

- Putting Principles into action

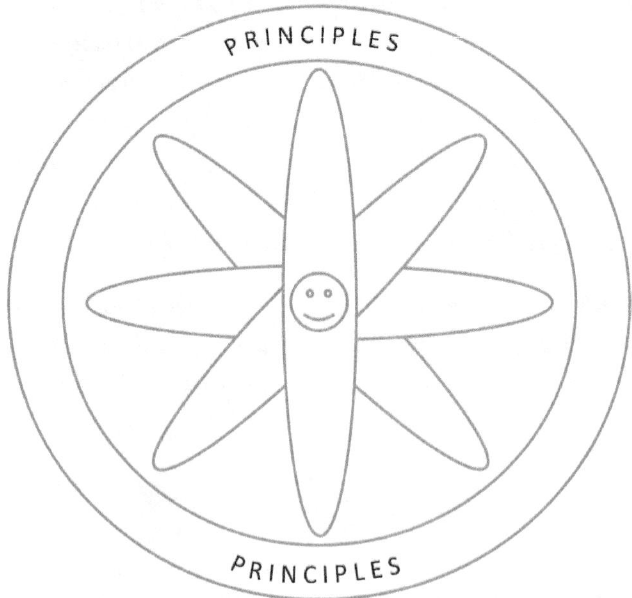

I am categorizing Principles under three heads:

- Laws of nature: For example, Newton's first law of motion – in an inertial frame of reference, an object either remains at rest or continues to move at a constant velocity, unless acted upon by a force.

- Laws created by humans for living in a predictable manner in the society.

- Ethics.

Laws of nature:

Even though no one has travelled to the sun, we know it's mass. Similarly, we know the mass of the planets and the moon. How? By using the law of gravity. In fact, we know that if you weigh 60 kilos on earth, you will weigh only 10 kilos on the moon.

These laws of nature govern what goes on in the universe and are followed by the universe. These laws are deduced from long-term observation of repeatable patterns and trends in nature. They are universal, uncovering behaviours that are true and verifiable across time and space. Faith or good intentions have nothing to do with these laws. We do not have a choice in obeying these laws.

Laws created by humans:

We humans are an unruly bunch, requiring laws to keep us in order, without which our society would become chaotic. These laws help control against the greed of our species. They also control individual and social behaviour, to make communal life less risky. These laws may vary from culture to culture, as these are based on moral values that lack global standards.

Laws tell us what we are required to do and what we are prohibited from doing. There are legal consequences or penalties for breaking them.

Ethics:

Ethics is different from law, especially those created by humans. Usually, laws set the minimum standard of behavior, while ethics set the maximum. Ethics are abstract guidelines that help people to decide what is right or wrong and how to act in certain situations. Ethics helps us make better choices for ourselves.

Ethical people demonstrate appropriate behavior in every facet of their life over time, even when their behaviour is not necessarily evident to others.

Ethics engages our mind and heart, thoughts and feelings. On one side, when you are ethical, you may have a sense of contentment. Conversely, you may sense remorse or guilt when you compromise your own standards. Ethics is determined by legal, individual, or professional norms. Ethics is a code of conduct, closer to ideal human character. Surpassing financial or legal impact, a breach or compromise of ethics usually results in loss of trust.

The legal process comes into focus when someone violates the law, whereas ethics is the conscience that comes into the fore when someone thinks of committing a violation.

To be in your Goldilocks Zone, it is important to adhere to Principles. Towards some (laws) you do not have a choice, and there are stringent implications for not adhering to these. The ones that do have a choice (ethics), are the ones that we need to imbibe in our way of thinking and day to day behavior. This requires a conscious effort every time we face a dilemma.

Laws do not tell us what to do in relation to many of the decisions we have to make in life. The goal is to not just comply, but move towards the 'maximum standards'. This includes holding everyone to the same standard, leading to a role model behavior that inspires others around you. Honesty, integrity, trust and fairness are all critical for an ethical person.

According to my research, the importance of being ethical increases with age, peaking around 51–55 years of age. In my opinion, after this phase, ethics becomes integrated into life.

How to be ethical?

Take a self-assessment of the following "Ethics Quotient" attributes. Rate each of them on a scale of 1 to 5. Please choose the number that best represents your feelings, thoughts and behaviours.

1	2	3	4	5
Less True				More True

S. No.	Statement	Your response
1.	I have defined my values and am aligned to them.	
2.	I know how I want to be remembered at the end of my life.	

S. No.	Statement	Your response
3.	I highly regard and demonstrate honesty and integrity.	
4.	I am inclusive.	
5.	I am approachable.	
6.	I empower others.	
7.	I prioritise people over profit.	
8.	I treat everyone well. I am conscious of bias and avoid bias.	
9.	I exercise empathy.	
10.	I act the way I would want others to act towards me (Treat others the way I would like to be treated).	
11.	I am open in my communication.	
12.	I am not afraid to speak up.	
13.	I think and do the right thing.	
14.	I feel a sense of duty.	
15.	I contribute to the betterment of others.	
16.	I do no harm through my actions or words.	
17.	I model ethical behavior consistently.	
18.	I consider myself trustworthy (I am reliable and dependable).	

Scoring: Please add up all 'Your responses' and review your "Ethics Quotient" in the Score Key.

Your "Ethics Quotient" Assessment

Score Key

Score Interpretation

Total Score: 73 – 90 — Ethical peak

This score indicates a high likelihood that you are demonstrating an ethical self in your thought and action. There are some aspects where you are still on the journey to be consistent.

Total Score: 37 – 72 — On the Ethical journey

This score indicates that you are on the path to being ethical. The aspects where you have scored low are the ones that you need to work on. You need to imbibe these in your way of thinking and day to day behavior.

Total Score: 18 – 36 — Yet to commence the Ethics journey

This score indicates a high likelihood that you have not started your ethics journey yet. The fact that you have taken this assessment is a positive indication of the commencement of the journey. All the aspects that you have scored low on are the ones that you need to work on. You need to imbibe these aspects in your way of thinking and day to day behavior.

Putting Principles into action

You could be flexible in many aspects, but when it comes to Principles there should be no compromise.

The statements in the Ethics assessment may seem short and simple but some of those statements need to be understood well for you to develop your action plan to be ethical. Here is a brief explanation of the key aspects:

Values:

Values are the motive behind purposeful action. They are the ends towards which we act. Personal values are personal beliefs about right and wrong and may or may not be considered moral. Ethical people know their core values and have the courage to abide by them in all areas of their lives, for the common good.

To help you identify your values and align to them, here are some examples of core values: commitment, compassion, courage, dependability, efficiency, fitness, good humor, honesty, innovation, loyalty, motivation, open-mindedness, optimism, patriotism, perseverance, respect, spirit of adventure, and service to others.

Some examples of values in action:

- Being a good steward of resources and in exercising frugality.

- Family is of fundamental importance.

- Honesty is always the best policy; trust has to be earned.

- Maintaining a healthy work/life balance.

Integrity:

Integrity refers to being honest and having a strong moral purpose. Ethical people demonstrate appropriate values to those around them via their own behavior. People generally connect more strongly with those whom they perceive as acting with integrity.

> Demonstrating integrity:
>
> - Keep promises and commitments and expect others to keep theirs.
>
> - Maintain loyalty towards those not present.
>
> - Apologize sincerely.
>
> - Act with honesty.
>
> - Take responsibility for your actions.

When it comes to integrity, you cannot follow what most people do; you need to do what is right.

Inclusiveness:

Inclusiveness is the achievement of an environment in which all individuals are treated fairly and respectfully, have equal access to opportunities and resources, and contribute fully to the collective success. At home or in personal interactions, how many times do we ask for a wider opinion or view before taking a decision? Whether it is our parents, spouse, children, friends or neighbours (anyone who is impacted by the decision). At work, inclusiveness is the creation of a work environment and culture that enables all employees to participate and thrive.

Demonstrating inclusiveness: Each person brings a unique perspective based on their unique life experiences. Respect and value that perspective.

Approachable:

Being approachable is a key to building relationships with people, and to create a strong bond in which trust, confidence and ideas can flow.

When you are approachable, people do not cover up problems but feel comfortable in sharing issues with you because they know that you will not react negatively.

Empower:

Empower means "give power or authority to". It is the giving or delegation of power or authorization; the giving of ability: enablement or permission.

The next time you are delegating something to your friend, spouse or child, see if you can share the big picture or objective, rather than telling them step by step what needs to be done.

In a work environment, empowerment is based on the belief that employees have the ability, and want to take on more responsibility.

Demonstrating empowerment: Give employees greater authority and responsibility to take care of the needs of customers/stakeholders and to provide employees with the means for making influential decisions. This should eliminate the "let me ask my boss" barrier by handing over a level of the decision-making power to front-line employees.

Bias:

Bias means a strong unreasoned inclination or a preconceived opinion about something or someone, in favour of or against something.

Many a time, we may not realize that we are acting in a biased manner. Unconscious bias occurs when people favour others who look like them and/or share their values. For example, a person may be drawn to someone with a similar interest, educational background, from the same area, or holding similar views. Bias can have an impact at work, especially when it comes to hiring, promotion, performance management, day to day meetings and behaviour.

How many times have you assumed that the pilot was male, or the person from your town would automatically become your friend, or that your best friend is always right?

Avoiding bias: Be aware of what it is, and how it can affect others, moving it from your subconscious into the conscious where you can manage the bias. To reduce the effects of bias, question biases in yourself and raise awareness in others.

An example of creating inclusive meeting practices (formal/informal, personal/official) –

- Acknowledge everyone at meetings

- Do not always sit next to the same person at every meeting.

- If you disagree with someone else's opinion respond constructively.

- Solicit the opinions of everyone at the meeting.

- Remember not to always draw upon the same people constantly.

Empathy:

Empathy is the ability to sense and understand people's emotions – whether in personal relationships or at work.

Empathy is a strength, more so in the workplace. It is your empathy that allows you to intuitively sense a colleague or customer's problem and suggest solutions or, recognize the stress in a team member and support him/her.

> Imbibing empathy:
>
> - Be sensitive to others' feelings and perspectives.
>
> - Take an active interest in their concerns.
>
> - Be attentive to emotional cues; listen deeply.
>
> - Be willing to change your mind or direction to accommodate others as long as the ethical foundation remains secure.
>
> - Be able to walk in someone else's shoes.

Communication:

In the context of principles and ethics, communication is about how we act to induce desirable and ethically grounded responses in others.

> Here are a few tips:
>
> - Cut ambiguity in your communication.
> - Clarify that you have been understood.

- Participate effectively in sharing and receiving ideas/perspectives.

- Deal with difficult issues in a straightforward manner.

- Welcome full sharing of information.

- Stay receptive to news – good or bad.

- Keep others informed.

Being trustworthy:

Being trustworthy is about how you maintain your personal commitment to an ethical life and how you are grounded in thought and action.

Demonstrating trustworthiness:

- Be reliable and dependable

- Be willing to admit mistakes

- Be true to your word and be worthy of others' confidence in you.

- Always keep your word.

Steps to deal with ethical dilemmas:

Identify potential situations that seem to attract ethical dilemmas. Recognizing when ethical dilemmas are likely to arise can help you be more attuned to the risk and to think carefully about how to behave with integrity.

Deal with ethical dilemmas as and when they arise.

- Prepare: Visualize how you might respond to various scenarios so you can think about the ethical aspects around such instances ahead of time.

- Evidence: Whenever possible, take time to carefully weigh all of the information you receive about a situation and assess if someone has actually acted in an unethical manner, before you react.

- Get advice: It is often helpful to talk through an ethical dilemma with a friend, mentor or even a spiritual advisor. Assessing advice rationally can help you to make important ethical decisions.

- Demonstrate courage: Sometimes you will need to make a decision that will leave you wondering afterwards, whether you did the right thing. These decisions can help you to learn to trust your instincts, release your anxiety and assess each situation logically rather than emotionally.

When faced with an ethical dilemma, think of those who adore you the most: would they be in agreement with your approach?

* * * * *

In a nutshell:

Principles provide us with a framework in life, to look back on, when we are in a dilemma about what is right or wrong. To be in your Goldilocks Zone, it's important to adhere to Principles and be on a path of self-discipline. The goal is to not just comply (with laws), but to move towards the 'maximum standards' (of ethics) and create a role model.

A key outcome for you, from this chapter, is to identify actions that you would like to take to develop your Principles – actions to help you be a role model. For example: You could start by taking actions from the Ethics Quotient Assessment.

Principles are the key behind building your life, career or organization. You can move the focus from good living standards to **living with good standards.**

In the next chapter, you will read about Purpose – the second step to be in your Goldilocks Zone.

* * * *

My acrylic painting version of Gautam Buddha, for whom sharing his knowledge about enlightenment with the world became his purpose.

To view the colour version, scan this QR code.

Chapter 5

Step 2 – Purpose

My grandfather was a freedom fighter. He wanted to become a doctor, and was in his late teens while doing his MBBS. One day, Mahatma Gandhi was visiting the town and was going to address a large gathering. My grandfather was keen on attending that speech. When the college principal, a Britisher, came to know of this, he called my grandfather and told him that he will be rusticated if he attended that meeting. My grandfather decided to attend that meeting, was rusticated from college, and thereafter spent the next couple of decades in the national freedom movement, and was jailed too.

The "turning point" in my grandfather's life was the conversation he had with his principal. That was when the purpose of his life became clear to him, and he took a decision that made his life's journey very clear and meaningful. He encountered the dilemma that changed the course of his life, for a change he wanted to bring to the people of the country. He later studied Law and leveraged the knowledge to help parties amicably settle cases out of court.

* * *

Astronomy has taught people about the vastness of the universe, about cosmos, space and how magnificent the stars are, how immense the Milky Way is, how the earth is just a small part of the much larger solar system and how we as humans, are like ants in this system. Yet humans have unique mental and emotional abilities that enable them to think and do certain things that other living beings cannot.

In the previous chapter, we looked at the different aspects related to Principles and delved into the need to be Ethical. In this chapter let us go through the journey of Purpose –

- What is Purpose?

- Why do you need a Purpose in life?

  o   Once you identify your Purpose, does it change?

  o   Does one have multiple Purposes or a single Purpose?

  o   What if you and your spouse have a different purpose?

  o   Why does it become difficult to find one's Purpose?

  o   Is happiness a Purpose?

- Do you know your Purpose? (Warming up exercise)

- Finding your Purpose

- How do you find your Purpose?

- Exercise: Explore your Purpose

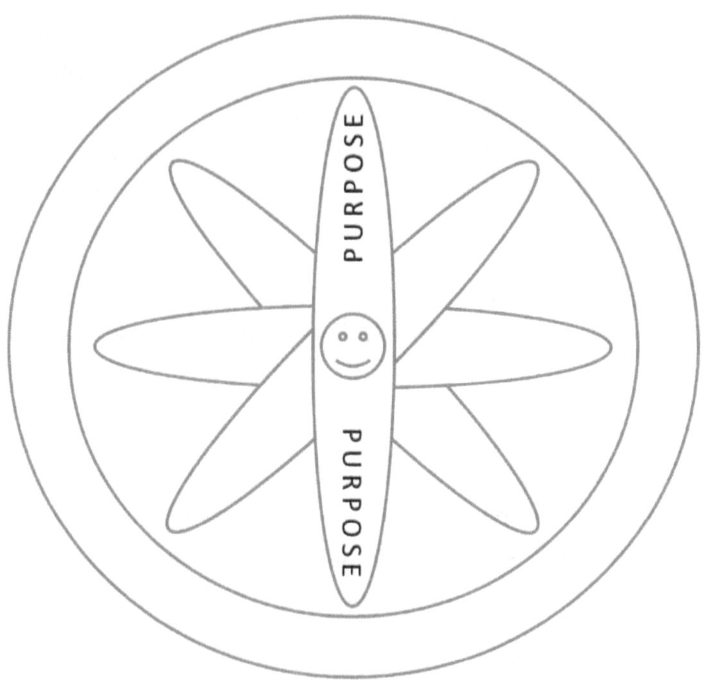

Let us start with 'Why' and then move on to the 'How' and the 'What'.

Purpose is about focusing on 'Why'. Why would you want to do whatever you want to do?

My father was passionate about Indian history and culture, and, as I grew up, he used to share many ancient Indian concepts with me. One such concept is about "*Puruṣārtha*", which literally means 'the aims of human life'.

According to this concept the four aims of a human life are – *Dharma* (righteousness, moral values), *Artha* (prosperity, economic values), *Kaama* (pleasure, desire, psychological values) and *Moksha* (liberation, spiritual values).

While all the four *"Purusarthas"* are important, in cases of conflict, *Dharma* is considered more important than *Artha* or *Kaama*. *Dharma* signifies duties, rights, laws, conduct, virtues – that are considered to make life possible. I would compare *Dharma* with Principles that I delved into in the previous chapter.

While *Dharma, Artha* and *Kaama* are aligned with an individual's social life, *Moksha* is aligned with an individual's spiritual life.

The ultimate ideal of human life is considered to be *Moksha*. *Moksha* signifies emancipation, liberation, release (freedom from the cycle of rebirth – for those who believe in the theory), self-knowledge, self-realization and achieving purity of mind. This is in a way comparable with the 'self-actualization' concept of Maslow.

The path to this ultimate ideal or **purpose of life** is via noble deeds – everything you do for the greater good that pushes you forward on the path of this ultimate purpose. That is where Passion, Skills and Strategy come into the picture (which we will elaborate upon in subsequent chapters). They address the 'What' and 'How', while Purpose addresses the 'Why'.

What is Purpose?

Purpose can be viewed as an intrinsically motivated framework for personally and socially meaningful goals that pull one into the future.

Definition of Purpose (Larissa Rainey, 2014, The Search for Purpose in Life): A consistent and central life aim that…

- draws upon one's unique strengths, talents, skills, values and passions,

- stimulates goals for the future that influence one's present actions,

- is at once personally meaningful and of contribution to someone or something outside the self

- is volitionally fulfilled (fulfilled using one's will).

The above points clearly elaborate how Purpose is a consistent and central life aim.

Manifesting divinity within: Swami Vivekananda was an Indian monk and a key figure in introducing Indian philosophies of Vedanta (one of the six orthodox schools of Indian philosophy) to the Western world during the late 19th century. Swami Vivekananda summarised the Vedanta as follows, giving it a modern and universalistic interpretation: each soul is potentially divine. The goal is to manifest this Divinity within through work and mental discipline – and be free. According to him, this is the whole of religion; rituals are secondary.

Why do you need a Purpose in life?

If this question has come up in your mind, then it indicates that you have some dissatisfaction with the way your life is progressing. Your life will be more streamlined if you align your life goals with your Purpose.

As human beings, we are all specially gifted with abilities of abstract thinking, rational thinking, imagination, self-reflecting consciousness, morality etc. Animals for example take actions based on their instincts. As infants we also act based on instincts. As our mental faculty grows, human beings develop the power to influence and create their destiny. Since we have this unique power, why not use it to identify and define our Purpose and work towards it.

Once you identify your Purpose, does it change?

Yes, your Purpose may change from time to time, depending on the stage of life you are in, your circumstances and maturity. It gradually becomes more distilled and focused.

Does one have multiple Purposes or a single Purpose?

You may start by having multiple Purposes. As you tread on the path of your Purpose – the reason for your being, the objective of your life usually starts to get refined to a single Purpose; one that is specific enough to provide direction, but broad enough to span life domains. It would act as a motivating, meaningful and beneficial resource for you to have in life.

What if you and your spouse have a different purpose?

It is not necessary that your spouse and you have a common purpose. Depending on situations, to accomplish each other's purpose, you may prioritise one over the other. You may together work on the first one and subsequently focus on the other. Adjustments are required in a relationship. This is in personal relationships. Similar adjustments may be required in relationships at work or in the society to prevent unhealthy conflicts.

I would like to share here as an example the adjustments my parents made after their wedding.

At the time of their wedding, my father was working in Mumbai, and my mother an MBBS doctor, was practicing medicine in Hyderabad. Post-wedding, they made a couple of adjustments. My father moved to Hyderabad, and my mother moved from active medical practice to a government job in the State Forensic Science Laboratory. This adjustment allowed my father to continue teaching and spend time on writing/journalism. For my mother, she had a wonderful career with the government job and retired as the first woman Director of that department.

Why does it become difficult to find one's Purpose?

People find it difficult to find their purpose in life because they hardly know themselves. They see themselves as who they think they are and how others see them. To know what you want in life, to know your purpose in life, *you* must know who you are.

Is happiness a Purpose?

We all want to be happy. While this may seem like a Purpose, it is actually the result of a worthy Purpose.

What could be the Purpose of life? Let's see below how you can create your own meaning and Purpose in life.

> The three facets below seem to bring together one's Purpose:
>
> - Find something important enough to make a positive difference.
>
> - Love others.
>
> - Leave a legacy. Leave the world a slightly better place.

Can these be brought further down to a few, simple words? From the examples that you have seen in this chapter and examples of people that you might be aware of, what seems like the apparent Purpose of our life is *to selflessly serve others.*

According to my research, the 55% respondents who had found the purpose of their life had the following words and phrases most commonly used in their purpose – Happy (65 respondents used the word), Life, Live, Make, Others, Family, Help, Healthy, People, Happiness, Love, Good (at least 10 respondents used the word). Below is the word-cloud:

one time world personal content will learn self give comes
Helping people Inspire create everyone successful
good person Live life world better place good peaceful
Happiness need healthy Lead happy family
create better version make satisfied life keep happy
career live successful person others fullest help
meaningful people around love good human purpose life
make surroundings help others helpful work achieve Serve children
change impact know service person able sure society way purpose

Do You Know Your Purpose? (Warming Up Exercise)

Let us warm up on the topic of 'your' Purpose! Take a self-assessment of the following attributes. Rate each of them on a scale of 1 to 5. Please choose one number that most of the times best represents your feelings, thoughts and behaviours.

| 1 | 2 | 3 | 4 | 5 |

Less True   More True

S. No.	Statement	Your response
1.	I know what I want to accomplish each day.	
2.	I prioritise important activities for the day (not just those that are urgent).	
3.	I decide on what is important for me to do and not let others decide that for me.	
4.	What I do each day adds up to what I want to accomplish in the long term.	
5.	I know why I want to do what I want to do or what I am doing.	
6.	I am aware of what activities give me the most satisfaction.	
7.	I am self-motivated to complete what I start.	
8.	I learn from my mistakes.	

S. No.	Statement	Your response
9.	I know well about my traits, strengths and capabilities.	
10.	I remain focused even in a distracting environment.	
11.	I know I have something meaningful to offer the world.	
12.	When encountered with an ethical dilemma I am comfortable in taking a stand that is unique.	
13.	I know what I care about.	
14.	I know what my values are.	
15.	I know what legacy I want to leave behind.	

Scoring: Please add up all "Your responses" and review your 'Do you know your Purpose' in the Score Key.

"Do you know your Purpose" Assessment

Score Key

Score Interpretation

Total Score: 60 – 75 — Clear about your Purpose

This score indicates a high likelihood that you know yourself quite well and you are clear about your Purpose. There are some aspects that you may still be exploring about yourself.

Total Score: 40 – 59 — On the journey of learning about yourself

This score indicates that you are on the journey of learning about yourself. The aspects/statements that you have scored low on are the ones that you need to explore more to understand more about yourself.

Total Score: 15 – 39 — Need to introspect

This score indicates a high likelihood that you have not embarked on your journey of learning about yourself. You need to invest time in introspection and self-reflection. All the aspects/statements that you have scored low on are the ones that you need to ponder more about.

Finding your Purpose

Take inspiration from others:

I read through the biographies of several well-known personalities and legends to understand what was the common thread running amongst them and their purpose in life. I have listed some of these personalities in the chapter: 'How to get into your Goldilocks Zone?'

> Some of the common themes amongst these legends are:
>
> - Turning point: There was a turning point in their lives where they took a decision that made their life's journey very clear and meaningful.
>
> - Turbulence: They encountered ethical dilemmas and decided to take a stand that was unique. People resonated with it and they had the moral support of the masses.
>
> - Transform: They used their capabilities for the benefit of people and in making the world a better place.

Turning points are a base for the 'Turbulence' and 'Transform' themes, and play a key role in finding your Purpose in life. These can be subtle or severe moments that have an impact on your approach towards life and take you on your unique journey. Some turning points are conscious decisions we take, while others may have been imposed by others. We may sometimes recognize turning points immediately and sometimes much later.

I am reminded of the situation that was a turning point in Mahatma Gandhi's life.

On 7 June 1893, as a young lawyer in a smart suit and holding a first-class train ticket, he was ordered to sit in third class, because of the colour of his skin. Gandhi refused and was forcibly removed from the train at Pietermaritzburg. He spent the night in the cold waiting room of the station. It marked a turning point in Gandhi's thinking and in his life. He felt that his dignity as an Indian and as a human being had been violated. After learning more about the position of the Indian community in South Africa and in the British Empire as a whole, Gandhi called for a peaceful protest against discriminatory laws. He founded the Natal Indian Congress in 1894.

We are all on our life journey with the potential to become a legend (and leave a legacy) in our own way, with our own turning point, turbulence in life, and the opportunity to "Be the change that you wish to see in the world." – Mahatma Gandhi.

A doctor friend of mine had seen the deaths of three close friends (during her childhood) due to the lack of proper healthcare facilities, resulting in her aspiration to become a doctor and provide good quality healthcare for children in her town. Quite similarly, I know of friends and relatives who had various experiences in their childhood or as they grew up, that resulted in their choice of careers and clarity of their life Purpose. The lack of educational opportunities for girls resulted in some people starting multiple schools and institutions for girls and women. Experiencing starvation resulted in a compassionate individual starting an NGO for distributing free food to the needy. Lack of good facilities for street children gave rise to building a home for them by philanthropic persons.

Here's an anecdote from my father's life, his turning point.

My father was born in the pre-independence phase when his father was mostly engaged in the national freedom movement. My father spent a lot of time with his grandparents and learnt the values of life, learnt about Indian political and literary personalities, history and culture. My father was the eldest amongst 11 siblings. After undertaking several family responsibilities and completing his studies, he moved to Mumbai to start a business with his brother. He soon realised that business was not his forte. He would rather spend his life sharing his knowledge. This was a "turning point" in his life, giving rise to a couple of key pursuits. Firstly, he started writing articles for newspapers and magazines, and eventually became a journalist. Secondly, he started teaching Hindi to senior school children, and alongside sharing his perspectives of life, values, history, culture and his interpretation of Indian rituals. He continued to do this for a good 50 plus years, even when he turned 90 and could barely see, he continued to dictate articles to be published on these topics. More than 300 articles and a couple of books have been published. Most of his students still remember him for the life stories that he shared with them in the classroom.

Sometimes Turning Points happen, but at other times we may need to take conscious actions to make them happen, in order to lead the life that we want to. These are those critical junctures in your life where decisions have a huge impact on your future. They occur every few years. These are times where you might want to consider consulting experienced people and take their guidance.

Some of the obvious points are – when you finish schooling and are going for higher studies in your area of interest (to specialize), this decision has an impact on your choice of career. The next point is when you move from the campus to the corporate world. The decisions at this stage have an impact on your foundation of work-related values. After you have worked for about a decade, you would want to reevaluate your path and your satisfaction with your life, and accordingly either change the path or make minor adjustments. After another ten years you will need to do a mid-career/mid-life assessment of your life purpose, again making changes or adding goals and objectives. This point is a critical one as it provides enough time for course correction, if required. Otherwise by the time you reflect on yourself, after another ten years, when you're almost fifty to fifty-five years old, you may undergo a lot of mental pressure trying to harmonize what you are doing with what you really want to do. At the next turning point, when you are about sixty-five, you are hopefully already doing what you wanted to do; otherwise you will need to make some drastic changes to be satisfied with the remaining journey of your life.

While the central purpose of your life may remain reasonably unchanged all through, there might be additional priorities depending on the phase of life you are in.

According to my research, 71% of the respondents knew what legacy they wanted to leave behind. Around 55% of the survey respondents had found the purpose of their life. The average age at which these respondents had found the purpose of their life was 34; the range as such varied between 13 and 57.

So, how do you find *your* Purpose?

It is important to reconcile with your past to integrate it into your present and future. One of Steve Jobs' famous quotes is about how various experiences in your life connect to become your aspired purpose: "You can't connect the dots looking forward; you can only connect them looking backwards. So, you have to trust that the dots will somehow connect in your future. You have to trust in something – your gut, destiny, life, *karma*, whatever."

You have now seen some of the common themes around the Purpose of life. The next steps are to review these aspects, reflect on your experiences, and invest time to find your unique Purpose. Answering the following questions will help you get closer to your Purpose:

- Context: What do you care about? What has stayed with you as an important aspect to address in life? What was possibly your subtle or severe turning point?

- Activity: What kind of activity gives you the most satisfaction? (Find something important enough to make a positive difference)

- Beneficiaries: For whom do you do this activity and what is the value these beneficiaries derive from you? (Love others)

- Result: How do your beneficiaries transform as a result of what you do for them? (Leave a legacy)

As you will notice in the above, 'Context' and 'Activity' are to do with yourself, whereas 'Beneficiaries' and 'Result' are to do with others. Those who have discovered their Purpose and acted on it focus on the people they serve.

For you to review an example, I am sharing my Purpose here:

Context: I believe that professionals who start working in companies are at a risk of falling into a routine that largely focuses on helping others accomplish their objectives, leaving them with a limited perspective on attaining their full potential in tune with their life goals and purpose. I went through this fast-paced journey myself, moving from one role to another, getting stuff done and accomplishing targets.

Activity: Coaching professionals gives me the most satisfaction (life coaching, executive coaching, and career transition coaching).

Beneficiaries: The beneficiaries of my coaching are professionals who are looking to explore their full potential. The value they derive from me is the support in achieving their professional and personal goals and living a life of purpose.

Result: As a result, they gain control of their life and achieve their most important goals. They get clearer about their goals and aspirations, about what they are capable of doing in order to achieve them and start moving closer to these by taking conscious action early in life.

Summary: Combining the above into one statement, my Purpose would be "Engaging with people to support them, explore their full potential in living a satisfying life."

Exercise: Explore your Purpose

Now it's your turn to explore your Purpose. To complete this exercise please sit in a place where you can focus, undisturbed.

Reflect on the questions below. Make rough notes in the space provided, of thoughts that come to your mind. Revisit some of the examples mentioned earlier in this chapter about turning points in people's lives. You can also reflect on turning points of those close to you – your parents, friends and relatives. Why are they doing what they are doing? What caused them to pursue a certain activity in a focused manner? Once you have noted your responses for the questions, review them a couple times, and try to draft your Purpose.

- Context: What do you care about? What has stayed with you as an important aspect to address in life? What was possibly your subtle or severe turning point?

____

____

____

____

____

- Activity: What activity gives you the most satisfaction? (Find something important enough to make a positive difference)

____

____

____

____

____

____

- Beneficiaries: For whom do you do this activity and what is the value these beneficiaries derive from you? (Love others)

____

____

____

____

____

____

- Result: How do your beneficiaries transform as a result of what you do for them? (Leave a legacy)

____

____

____

____

____

____

- Summary: Combining the above into one statement, your Purpose would be "_______________________

____

____

____

____

__________________________________"

* * * * *

In a nutshell:

 When you do not know what your Purpose is, then you are essentially living someone else's Purpose instead of your own, possibly leading to dissatisfaction in life.

To be in your Goldilocks Zone, understand *your* Purpose – a combination of finding something important enough to make a positive difference in your life and that of others, love for others, and leaving a legacy behind. Simply put – something you do to selflessly serve others.

Once you identify your purpose, your thoughts, emotions and actions, start getting focused towards your purpose, and you will get up every morning eager to fulfill your Purpose and every experience (good or bad) that day will help take you closer to your Purpose. This will help you to not just 'make a living' but actually 'live your life'.

A key outcome for you, from this chapter, is to gain clarity in your Purpose of life –

- Context (What do you care about?)

- Activity (Doing what activity gives you the most satisfaction?)

- Beneficiaries (For whom do you do this activity and what is the value they derive from you?)

- Result (How do your beneficiaries transform as a result of what you do for them?)

How you think, what you do, how you live, all get aligned to your life's Purpose.

In the next chapter you will read about Passion– the third step to be in your Goldilocks Zone.

* * * * *

My acrylic painting depicting the happiness & satisfaction from being on the path of one's passion.

To view the colour version scan this QR code.

Chapter 6

Step 3 – Passion

A friend of mine, Vikram, passionate about writing, was an internal communications expert. He lost his job during the pandemic.

The communications that he developed at work were always driven by the key messages required to be communicated in the corporate environment. He started to reach out to several corporate organisations, writing to them in many creative ways about himself, but the market was dull, and he could not land himself a job. Each night he would write a blog on how he was keeping himself sane in those times, lessons learnt in life, remaining optimistic, online courses he was taking up, taking care of physical and mental health and other similar topics. He soon garnered a huge following, and a few people started to reach out to him for short-term content writing assignments. Soon he was more than busy working on several such parallel assignments.

He became a full-time freelancer; choosing topics that were close to his heart, doing what he was passionate about, and helping people communicate their ideas better.

* * *

As the astronomer needs to go much above the earth to understand several phenomena about it, you also need to go

87

above your routines to understand the driving energy behind you, your purpose and your passion.

You have so far explored two steps – Principles and Purpose. In this chapter let us explore Passion. We shall look at the following:

- What is Passion?

- Why do you need to know what your Passion is?

- How do you find your Passion?

When youngsters are at the start of their careers and are making a choice, their near and dear prefer careers where there is more money, social respect, predictability, stability, potential growth etc. What is more important in choosing a career is one's passion.

Sometimes, as a youngster one may not be able to make the best choice based on one's passion. But starting with what is close to your heart is an important aspect. The next aspect to consider is the economic potential associated with what one is passionate about. You must have heard of the old saying "Follow your passion, and success will follow you." These choices need to be re-evaluated based on changing circumstances and developments in life. One's passion can change with age, depending on one's priorities during a particular stage in life. So, this is not just an issue for those at the start of their careers, it can also be a problem for those trapped for years in doing something that they are not passionate about.

Passion is not just about social causes like propagating education, healthcare, sanitization, supporting the girl child, clean drinking water, public transportation, waste management, environment protection, electricity, women safety, infrastructure, poverty, population, concern for animals etc. All of these are very important. You can be passionate about propagating art, dance or music, designing convenience products, innovating in a long-established area, forming an association, or be passionate about healthcare and fitness solutions. What one is passionate about is very personal to each person.

Choosing a job or a career because others have been successful at it, because of the money in it, because of its popularity, or because your family members prefer it, should not be the primary motivation for the choice. Money is important in life but it cannot buy time. So do not waste your life doing something you are not passionate about, just for the money you can earn. You do not have to feel guilty to do what you are passionate about. If you choose a career that you are passionate about then the chances are high that you will do wonders in that area and logically, money, respect, fame, satisfaction, will follow.

When you do what you are passionate about, you will wake up in the morning eager to jump out of your bed to get going and do what you love.

Sometimes in life, we may have to be passionate about what we do, than get to do early what we are passionate about. However, it doesn't mean that you can never do what you are passionate about. If you have an idea of what you are passionate about then take one small step towards it at a time. It is never too late. Each step will take you closer to your passion. Nothing in your life goes waste; every step is like a dot. One of the ways to also discover your passion is to connect the dots. You shall see more on this topic later in this chapter.

Can you be passionate about multiple aspects?

Sure, you can. You could be passionate about fitness, about baking, about supporting a not for profit/NGO, providing them marketing support to generate funds, about travelling across the world, about writing/blogging. You could pursue them all together, though you might prioritise one over the other, or dedicate more time to one over the other. In fact Passion evolves with time; based on what influences you, what you have learnt, your experiences, and exposure.

Amongst the Why, What, and How of being in your Goldilocks Zone, Passion answers the 'What'. But what is Passion?

What is Passion?

Passion is that which you are willing to suffer for. The price you are personally willing to pay for something you desire. The challenges you would love to face in pursuit of your passion. The pain you are willing to endure to accomplish what you are passionate about.

I am passionate about drawing and painting. I never get tired when I am painting. My wife has told me several times to rest. For me, I am resting when I am painting. I find time on weekends to paint; it is a good way for me to relax after a busy week. I feel that it helps me to be more creative at work and in other aspects of my life. I can sacrifice sleep, I can miss out on a good movie, I can continue without eating or drinking, I can spend the entire weekend just drawing and painting. I visit art galleries and art exhibitions. I spend hours researching on painting techniques and then practicing them. Each painting is unique to me as it is an outcome of certain emotions behind it. People who see the paintings are sometimes appreciative, sometimes critical and sometimes indifferent. None of the reactions bother me; I pick what I value, as I am on my own journey, not on someone else's.

Those who are passionate about fitness, make time to hit the gym each day, rain or sunshine. They even make sure they do not miss their exercise regime when they are traveling or are on a holiday. Asking them to take a break would be akin to tying them to a chair.

Suffering is an essential aspect for something you are passionate about and when you pursue something that is meaningful to you.

Let me share with you a personal example of what I realized I was not passionate about.

Several years ago, I had the urge to learn a musical instrument and I started taking formal piano lessons. Since I was busy on weekdays, I had two back-to-back forty-five minute classes on Saturdays. Over three years I successfully completed the Trinity syllabus for Initial and Grade 1, and was preparing for Grade 2 tests. I was supposed to practice on the piano for 30–60 minutes each day, but was unable to. I used to sense a pressure building in me on Thursday night to practice the pieces in preparation for the class on Saturday. One Saturday I just did not feel like going to the class anymore and I gave it up. I realized I was not passionate about learning the piano. Actually, that is when I consciously started pursuing drawing and painting which I have loved ever since I was a kid.

Some years ago, I visited an engineering college to interact with students. It was a session organised to bridge the gap between the employers and students (tomorrow's talent market). I asked a few students why they were doing that specific engineering course. Quite a few of them told me that their parents were eager to see them become engineers. This is in their late teens. Often this situation of living for others' dreams continues for several years until one day they discover their purpose of life, their passion, and how they can do what *they* want to do.

Let's look at what makes up Passion.

Passion…

- is what you are willing to sacrifice lesser pleasures in life for.

- puts you into action; your life revolves around it, it motivates you.

- challenges you to continuously improve at what you are passionate about.

- takes you closer to *your* purpose of life.

Let us get a better understanding of each of the aspects that make up Passion.

'Willing to sacrifice' is about prioritizing and doing what you are passionate about, to gain long-term satisfaction, against other activities that may provide short term happiness.

Action: life revolves around it, motivates you, it is about your passion taking center-stage. All your activities, decisions, daily routine, tasks, associations, etc., start to focus around what you are passionate about. It motivates you each day, and at times you unknowingly also take action out of your comfort zone.

You are bound to have the natural urge to continuously improve and excel at something you are passionate about. The world may be happy with you being good at something, but you excel at what you are passionate about, to set a new benchmark for yourself.

The path to your purpose of life is via noble deeds, while the 'Purpose' is about 'Why' and Passion is about the 'How'.

Passion takes you closer to your purpose of life, helping to carry it out. Your passion is your reason for jumping out of bed each morning to move closer to your purpose in life.

Why do you need to know what your Passion is?

According to my research, people 'seem' to have a good understanding (5.3 on 7) of their passion in their early days (18 – 30 years). This understanding then takes a dip (4.7 on 7) and starts to increase, with the maximum clarity (6.1 on 7) in the age-group of 51–55.

Your life is not long enough to waste in doing something you do not feel strongly about. Once you know what gets your juices flowing, then work will not seem like drudgery; you will be energetic and perform with enthusiasm; hurdles will not stop you. You will become more closely aligned with your purpose.

You can move from just surviving to thriving in life.

There will be activities you need to do that you may not be passionate about. While it is acceptable to spend time on some activities which may drain you, the proportion of those should not outweigh the activities you love. If you love your weekends because that is the only time you get to pursue your passion and dislike your weekdays because the job you do only helps you pay your bills, then that is an unhealthy ratio.

A friend of mine is a graphic designer, whose passion is to animate, be creative and come up with interesting visuals. He loves photography and sketching too. At work this is what he does. For him his vocation is what he enjoys most. He can relate more meaningfully to what he does and come up with superior concepts and ideas.

Passion brings a lot of hidden energy with it.

When you do what you are passionate about, time just flies past without causing any strain on you. You continue to feel energized and perform enthusiastically. On the contrary, doing what does not trigger your passion will most likely lay stress on your mind and body, thereby creating health issues in the long run.

Hurdles do not stop you. When you are impassioned about what you do, you take on the challenges and obstacles that come your way, with a positive mindset and find innovative solutions to address them.

Being fervent about work does not necessarily mean it makes you happy but rather that it is meaningful – that it helps see things beyond the immediate situation. Doing something you are zealous about leads you to a more satisfying and fulfilling life. The work you do is not just leveraging your mental and physical abilities but is also backed by your emotions, taking you closer to living your purpose.

Reflecting back on the concept of *"Puruṣārtha"*, in the context of this book and the Goldilocks Zone, I think *Moksha* aligns with the ultimate objective of life, practically with the purpose of selflessly serving others. While *Kaama* aligns with doing what you are passionate about. To 'do it' you need to explore your passion.

How do you find your Passion?

You can find your passion with this exercise which will further build on the exercise you completed in the previous chapter on exploring your Purpose.

Exercise: Finding your Passion

Take a sheet of paper, and start writing down aspects that you are Passionate about. Write down anything that comes to mind. Browse through all the topics/questions mentioned below and write down your responses. Feel free to leverage your mind, heart and intuition. Once you have got them all listed, evaluate them and identify the top three to five aspects that you are passionate about. This exercise involves a lot of effort but it will be worth the investment.

Step 1 is to review your responses to the exercise on exploring your Purpose, covering the Context (what you care about, your turning point); Activity (doing what activity gives you the most satisfaction, something important enough to make a positive difference); Beneficiaries (whom do you do this activity for and what is the value these beneficiaries derive from you); Result (how your beneficiaries transform as a result of what you do for them); Summary (your statement of purpose).

Step 2 is to browse through all the topics/questions mentioned below and write down your responses. There is space available on subsequent pages for each question, for you to jot down your responses.

Questions:

Who are you? (Inputs from your past) What do you like doing? (Inputs from others)

- **Who are you? (Not who you want to be)**

    o   What is your personality style? Use MBTI or similar assessments to understand your personality style, preferences and behaviors, if you have not already taken one. (MBTI combinations come from your preferences towards: Extraversion/Introversion; Sensing/Intuition; Thinking/Feeling; Judging/Perceiving). (The Myers-Briggs Personality Type Indicator is a self-report inventory designed to identify a person's personality type, strengths, and preferences. The questionnaire was developed by Isabel Myers and her mother Katherine Briggs based on their work with Carl Jung's theory of personality types. Today, the MBTI inventory is one of the most widely used psychological instruments in the world).

o   What are your Strengths? Use the Strength Finder assessment (by Tom Rath) if you would like. (The StrengthsFinder Assessment was originally published in 1998 by Gallup and was written by Tom Rath. The book provides you with details for 34 strength themes. Once you complete the 30-minute assessment you get a report that ranks and details your top five strength themes).

o   What energises you? This relates to activities that strengthen you, drawing you in and energizing you. ("Now, Discover Your Strengths" by Marcus Buckingham, Donald O. Clifton is based on a massive Gallup study. This book shows individuals how to cultivate their own strengths and how to capitalize the talents of others.)

o   What do you love doing? What is that thing for which you are willing to sacrifice lesser pleasures in life, bear the pain, for which you are willing to face challenges and hurdles – that which will not stop you from pursuing them, for which you do not mind being embarrassed?

o   What drains you? (What you do not prefer doing, something that drains your energy and weakens you)

o   Who are your role models and why? Who inspires you and for what?

- **Inputs from your past**

o   What did you enjoy doing as a kid while growing up, and why?

o   Amongst all previous jobs/assignments that you have done, what are the common threads/themes – why did you do those jobs, what did you like in them (any common threads there)?

o   For what aspects are you a go-to person? What do people come to you for guidance/help/ support for?

- **What do you like doing?**

o   Things that you do most often by choice; while you are doing it, time flies by; your hobbies.

o   Type of subjects/topics you like to read about/ know about.

o   Create an imaginary bucket-list with an assumption that you have no financial constraint. After you finish doing everything on that bucket-list what would you still want to continue doing?

o   What do you/would you volunteer time for?

o   What do you want to get better at (improve/learn/ invest time in)?

- **Inputs from others**

    o   Ask others for inputs about what they think you are passionate about.

Step 3: Based on the exercise done so far, identify an initial list of areas that you are passionate about, without worrying about any limit. Then evaluate that list and identify the top three to five aspects that you are passionate about.

There is space below each step for you to make notes.

Step 1: Review your summary statement of purpose, especially your turning point.

____

____

____

____

____

Step 2: Who are you (not who you want to be)?

- What is your personality style? Use MBTI or similar assessments to understand your personality style, preferences and behaviour.

____

____

____

- What are your Strengths? Use the Strength Finder assessment (Tom Rath) if you would like to find your top five strengths.

____

____

____

____

- What energizes you? This relates to your strengths – activities that strengthen you, drawing you in, energizing you (Marcus Buckingham).

____

____

____

____

- What do you love doing? What are you willing to sacrifice lesser pleasures in life for, to bear the pain, for which you are willing to face challenges and hurdles – that will not stop you from pursuing them, for which you do not mind being embarrassed (because you want to continue learning about that aspect)?

____

____

____

____

- What drains you? (What you do not prefer doing, that drains your energy, that weakens you)

  ____

  ____

  ____

  ____

- Who are your role models, and why? Who inspires you, for what?

  ____

  ____

  ____

  ____

Inputs from your past.

- What did you enjoy doing as a kid and while growing up, and why?

  ____

  ____

  ____

  ____

- Amongst all previous jobs/assignments that you have done, what are the common threads/themes – why did you do those jobs, what did you like in them (any common threads there)?

  ____

  ____

  ____

  ____

- For what aspects are you a go-to person? For what do people come to you for guidance/help/support?

____

____

____

____

What do you like doing?

- Things that you do most often by choice; while you are doing it, time flies by; your hobbies.

____

____

____

____

- Type of subjects/topics you like to read about/know about.

____

____

____

____

- Create an imaginary bucket-list with an assumption that you have no financial constraints. After you finish doing everything on that bucket-list what would you still want to continue doing?

____

____

____

____

- What do you/would you volunteer time for?

____

____

____

____

- What do you want to get better at (improve/learn/ invest time in)?

____

____

____

____

Inputs from others.

- Ask others for inputs about what they think you are passionate about. Sometimes those closest to us can see things we might not be able to see ourselves. Ask them the question, "What do you think I am passionate about?" Please remember to give them time to respond, do not rush them on this.

____

____

____

____

Step 3: Based on the exercise done so far, identify an initial list of areas that you are passionate about, without worrying about any limit:

____

____

____

____

Now evaluate the above list and identify the top three to five aspects that you are passionate about.

____

____

____

____

As an example, someone's initial list might look like this:

- Giving back to the community.

- Supporting street children to achieve their dreams.

- Keeping my group of support workers motivated to help me with my passion in supporting street children.

- Earning enough money to support myself, my family and for charity.

- Traveling around the globe, sightseeing and visiting friends and relatives.

- Being adventurous and experiencing adventure sports.

- Living in a beautiful home with a loving family.

- Keeping fit and healthy.

- Enjoying a wide variety of food.

- Being a famous writer/author about travel.

- Having global visibility of my work and being globally recognized for it.

From the above, top four shortlisted/identified areas that the person is passionate about might look like these:

- Supporting street children to achieve their dreams.

- Being a famous writer/author about travel.

- Traveling around the globe.

- Keeping fit and healthy.

* * * * *

In a nutshell:

To be in your Goldilocks Zone, understanding what you are passionate about is critical. Your 'Purpose' answers the question of 'Why' about your life, 'Passion' answers the 'What'; what is close to your heart, what you are willing to make sacrifices for. Passion puts you into action; your life revolves around it. It keeps you motivated in life and challenges you to continuously improve. Passion takes you closer to *your* purpose of life.

A key outcome for you, from this chapter, is to have identified the top three to five aspects that you are passionate about – leveraging your Purpose and responses to questions on, "Who are you?"

If you had challenges in figuring out your 'purpose' then leverage the exercise you did to find your 'passion' to explore your 'purpose'.

Also note that if you are jumping to explore your Passion before understanding the Purpose of your life, then it appears like you want to travel without knowing why.

Do you need a mentor/coach?

According to my research, 74% of respondents felt the need for someone to support them to be more satisfied in life and not just to gain a successful career. A mentor/coach was the most sought-after person after a family member or friend.

In the next chapter you will read about Skills – the fourth step to be in your Goldilocks Zone.

* * * *

My acrylic painting of the Rameshwaram Temple corridor depicting the intricate design, architecture and skill.

To view the colour version scan this QR code.

Chapter 7

Step 4 – Skills

My son studied in a school that had a swimming pool. He had a weekly swimming class as part of his curriculum. He learnt to swim when he was seven. On weekends he would want to swim.

I did not know how to swim, neither did my wife. So we were reluctant to take him to the club to swim. Then we realised that this was a great opportunity for us to learn too. And we did just that – in our early thirties! Skills can be learnt. There needs to be a desire.

* * *

When you look at the earth from a distance, you can see water and portions of land, but there are certainly no national boundaries visible. These are political – man-made. In the same way you need to rise beyond your self-created boundaries in what you can achieve, by assessing your skills and capabilities.

You have so far explored three steps to be in your Goldilocks Zone – Principles, Purpose and Passion. Principles address the aspects around the framework of morals and ethics. Purpose addresses the 'Why'. Passion and Skills address the 'What'.

In the previous chapter you have delved deep into the aspects of Passion. In this chapter let's explore your Key Skills. We shall look at the following:

- Why do you need to know about your key skills?

- What are skills?

- How do you find your key skills?

- Exercise to relate Skills to your Passion.

The path to your purpose of life is paved with your passion and skills – doing what you are passionate about, leveraging your key abilities, matching your true gifts and potential, maximising the abilities you were born with. Your awareness about your passion helps you to effectively identify the required skills, to accomplish what you want to do.

Why do you need to know about your key skills?

You require skills to be able to do what you are passionate about. If you are passionate about something, then you might already have the necessary skills to pursue it.

Sometimes we are passionate about something but do not have the associated skills, or have them at a very foundational level. The good thing is that skills can be learnt. So if you are passionate about writing, then you can attend classes and learn the techniques, brush up your skills, or enhance them and get on with your journey.

Interestingly, apart from learning and improving yourself, skills can also be complemented by others. If you are passionate about something but you do not have those skills, then you could hire those skills, borrow them or even outsource them. I know a family that is passionate about helping people go through regular health checkups to scan for early symptoms of health issues. They regularly organize health camps and invite pathologists and doctors to support them in the cause.

What are Skills?

Skills include natural abilities that you have along with knowledge and capabilities that you have acquired through experience and learning.

Skills are your ability to do certain activities, and deliver results within a defined use of time and effort. Skills are abilities you have learned, practiced and/or have experience doing.

Skills can be categorized as follows:

- Personality based

- Aptitude based

- Knowledge based

Personality based skills: These are skills that are a result of your personality characteristics that contribute to how you perform activities. These might have been acquired through your experiences and your upbringing, or developed since childhood. These are related to your personality style, depending on whether you are an outgoing or reserved person; result-oriented or relationship-oriented person; fast-paced or slow-paced. Examples: decisive, logical, methodical, detail-oriented, empathic, imaginative.

Aptitude based skills: These are skills that are action oriented. For example: planning, communication, problem-solving, initiative, teamwork, writing, organizing. These can also be termed as soft skills. There might be some skills that you can leverage across areas that you are passionate about, making them 'transferable skills'.

Knowledge based skills: These are skills that are based on the knowledge you have acquired on specific subjects through work experience, training programs or formal education. These can also be termed as "hard skills"; these can be tested and may include technical or academic qualifications. Examples: marketing, accounting, programming, designing, animation, analytics.

The proficiency level of skills may range from being at an initial or foundational level, to an advanced level, and moving up to an expert or mastery level.

You may apply or leverage skills based on the proficiency in different ways. Let's say your passion is to be a motivational speaker, and the key skill you leverage is your skill in communication. In your childhood or adolescence, you might have done well at school in elocutions or debates; your skill might have been at a foundational level. As you started to work, you might have leveraged the skill to conduct training workshops or make remarkable presentations. This is where the skill was leveraged by you to accomplish some results, and it might have been at a more advanced level then. As you further improve your special skill, you might have started using it to coach and mentor individuals, helping and supporting them. Finally, at some stage in your life you might turn to become a motivational speaker, leveraging this skill to address a large number of people and their concerns. At this stage your communication skills might be at the expert or mastery level.

Performing a skills inventory assessment for yourself will help you understand what you are good at, what your key skills are, if you have the adequate/appropriate skills to pursue your passion, if you need to put in action a development plan, or if you need to complement these skills in some other way.

I am listing these same points below so you can focus on each of them.

A skills inventory assessment will help you understand the following:

- What are you good at, what are your key skills?

- Do you have the adequate/appropriate skills to pursue your passion? Are there gaps, if so, what are those gaps?

- Do you need to put a development plan into action?

- Do you need to complement these skills in some other way? How?

Average skills situation: Let us say for example, if you are passionate about something, for which you need a certain set of skills,. But are not an expert in any of them, and are just average in those skills.

Sometimes, just leveraging these combined average skills might enable you to pursue your passion. Say you are an average artist and an average computer programmer. You may find it challenging to have your own art exhibition or become an ace programmer soon. But, if your passion is to become a computer animation expert, then you might already have the right mix of skills.

A variation: Say you are an average artist and an average analyst. You may find it challenging to have your own art exhibition too soon, or become a generic analyst. But, if your passion is to become an art critique then you might already have the right mix of skills.

How do you find your key Skills?

Here are steps to go about finding your key skills.

As you start going through these steps, keep in mind that apart from doing a self-analysis you can also take inputs about your key skills from your managers/supervisors, friends, colleagues, teachers/professors, stakeholders and others who have worked closely with you on some assignments.

- Step 1: Identify your personality-based skills; skills that are a result of your personality characteristics. These are innate to your way of thinking and doing things.

Examples: decisive, logical, methodical, detail-oriented, empathic, imaginative etc.

- Step 2: Identify your aptitude-based skills; skills that you know you are good at, skills that you have used effectively at work, on assignments, might have received positive feedback for from your colleagues or supervisors, been awarded or recognized for. Examples: planning, communication, problem-solving, initiative, teamwork, writing, organizing.

- Step 3: Identify your knowledge-based skills. Create a list based on your educational background, certifications you may have undertaken, training workshops you may have attended, aspects in which you have work-experience. Examples: marketing, accounting, programming, designing, animation, analytics, project management etc.

- Step 4: Review the list of skills that you have created from step 1 to 3 and expand the list by adding related skills that come to your mind.

- Step 5: Review the entire list of skills that you have created and look for a correlation amongst the skills. Group your skills into logical themes.

- Step 6: Now choose your top five key skills and list them.

Space is provided below for you to make notes for the exercise.

Step 1: Identify your personality-based skills.

____

____

____

____

Step 2: Identify your aptitude-based skills.

____

____

____

____

Step 3: Identify your knowledge-based skills.

____

____

____

____

Step 4: Review the list of skills that you have created from step 1 to 3 and expand the list by adding related skills that come to your mind.

____

____

____

____

Step 5: Review the entire list of skills that you have created and look for a correlation amongst the skills. Group your skills into logical themes.

____

____

____

____

____

Step 6: Now choose your top five key skills and list them.

____

____

____

____

____

Exercise to relate your Skills and Passion:

At this point where you have analysed and identified your key skills, it is important to relate your key skills to your passion. The following five steps will help you do that.

Step 1: Reflect on the aspects you are passionate about. Refer to the outcome of the exercise from the previous chapter – the top three to five aspects that you are passionate about.

____

____

____

____

____

Step 2: What are the key skills required to do what you are passionate about? List them out.

____

____

____

____

____

____

Step 3: List your key skills and rate them on your proficiency level (Basic/Advanced/Expert).

____

____

____

____

Step 4: Assess the gap between the skills that are required for you to do what you are passionate about and your key skills. Are there additional skills that you need to develop your competency in?

____

____

____

____

Step 5: If there is a gap then how do you plan to address that gap? (You may need more space for this section.)

____

____

____

____

____

The table below summarises the exercise to relate your Skills and Passion:

Areas you are Passionate about	Skills required to do what you are Passionate about (A)	Your key skills and proficiency		Skill gap (A-B)	Actions to address the gap
		Skills (B)	Proficiency		

* * * * *

In a nutshell:

 To be in your Goldilocks Zone, doing what you are passionate about is critical. Your key skills help you accomplish this.

A vital outcome for you from this chapter is to identify your top five skills (personality based, aptitude based and knowledge based) and relate your Skills and Passion – assess the gap between the skills that are required for you to do what you are passionate about and your key skills, and develop a plan to address the gap (if there is one).

If you had challenges in figuring out your passion, then leverage the exercise you did to find your key skills to explore your passion. The themes emerging from your list of skills can give you a good perspective on where your passion lies.

In the next chapter you will read about Strategy – the fifth step to be in your Goldilocks Zone.

* * * *

My crayon drawing of our memorable trip to Venice, as part of a very well planned and executed trip to Greece and Italy.

To view the colour version scan this QR code.

Chapter 8

Step 5 – Strategy

Imagine you are in Mysore visiting the Mysore Palace on Dushera, one of the most beautiful celebrations of this city. On your drive to Bangalore, you bump into a tourist who talks about the wonderful road trip they had to Ladakh from Delhi a few months ago. You seriously start considering the possibilities of this trip for the next year.

This gives you about six months to plan and make it happen. There is a lot to do. You need to understand the driving route, the vehicle required, the good hours of practice required, getting physically fit for it, the en route stop overs, find out who can help, activate your network, get your friends to join, plan travel requirements, reservations, and many such tasks.

Sometimes six months might seem too short given the preparation required, especially if you are planning a road trip.

Now imagine you started thinking about this only in March and you had just a couple of months to prepare. You could still make it happen by making several compromises. The worst of them could be about the road trip itself, changing it to flying into Ladakh or many other not so ideal changes.

Our life is quite like that. The earlier you know what you want to do, the more time you have to properly plan, execute and get to enjoy the journey to the fullest.

* * *

123

When we think of outer space it seems like It is very far. But if you think of driving to space, you could get there in about an hour in your car, provided you could drive straight up into the sky! You may also face some traffic of aeroplanes cutting across you within the first fifteen minutes. Your goal may seem distant till the time you develop a strategy and implement it.

Strategy is the fifth and last of the steps to be in your Goldilocks Zone. Principles address aspects around the framework of morals and ethics. Purpose addresses the 'Why'. Passion and Skills address the 'What', and Strategy addresses the 'How'.

In this chapter we shall look at the following:

- What is a Strategy?

- Why do you need a Strategy?

- How do you go about creating your Strategy?

- How do you go about effectively implementing your action plan?

It is obvious that if you do not know your destination then you cannot reach it. Now that you have gone through the journey of understanding Principles, identifying your Purpose, Passion and key Skills, you are ready to develop your personal Strategy to be in your Goldilocks Zone.

Yes, the prerequisite to this step is to have completed the exercises to have clarity about the previous four steps and leverage those insights about you in developing an effective strategy.

What is a Strategy?

Strategies help in solving problems, doing something new or making a change happen, considering the long-term and the big picture perspective. There are several ways to explain strategy. I found this quote quite relevant to the context of this book. "Strategy is the path you will take towards meeting your goals and fulfilling your vision." – Kristina Halvorson.

Strategy is a tool to help you turn your thoughts and ideas around your Purpose, Passion and Skills into reality. It tells you how you can accomplish what you want to accomplish. It is the overarching method or path chosen for achieving your objectives.

For your benefit, we will also get down to developing specific action plans. What is important to remember is that your strategy can be updated and modified in tune with your awareness of yourself, your needs and your changing environment at any time.

What should your personalized strategy cover? It should ideally cover the following aspects:

- The challenge/objectives: This is a result of your soul-searching and introspection, as well as evaluating the current and possible future environment, leading to the objective of accomplishing your Purpose of life, by doing what you are Passionate about and leveraging your key Skills.

    o   State your Purpose

    o   State your Passion

    o   State your key skills

- Considerations for your strategy: This is the way of working guidance that you will refer to frequently, and based on your analysis of situations, revisit your action plan if required.

    o   Engaging and communicating with stakeholders

    o   Barriers

    o   Resources

    o   Opportunities

    o   Balancing the urgent and important

- Action plan: This is where you develop and include detailed plans for each objective (or challenge) to be achieved in a defined timeframe. Include description of milestones. You should regularly review and track the plans and milestones to check whether the progress is satisfactory and if you are meeting the desired expectations and to identify any course correction required.

    o   Action(s) to accomplish an Objective, Support required, Timelines to start and complete actions.

These aspects will be delved deeper into in the latter section of this chapter – 'How do you go about creating your Strategy?'

Why do you need a Strategy?

According to my research, people rated the statement "I am aware of what skills I need, to do what I am passionate about" 5.4 on a 7 point scale, and 5.8 on 7 for the statement "I would learn skills to be satisfied in life". "I have invested time and energy in developing a strategy to accomplish my life's purpose" was rated 4.6 on 7.

What this means is that people might know what skills they need to fulfill their passion and would also want to learn those skills, but have not invested enough in developing a strategy to do this.

Further, fewer people seem to have been able to successfully implement their strategy to accomplish their life's purpose till the age of 40 (3.9 on 7). Whereas, there is an increased amount of strategy implementation in the 41 – 55 phase of life (4.6 on 7). One of the prime objectives of this book is to help you start implementing your strategy to accomplish your life's purpose early in life.

We have all attended some wonderful self-development session or the other – workshops, conferences, speeches, motivational talks, transformational seminars etc. Imagine you are attending one on Friday. The training session starts on a low key, gradually you see a lot of value in the content, there are several aha moments, you make a lot of notes, you do a lot of exercises, you are mesmerized by the trainer, you are all energized to take all the learning to your workplace. As your weekend starts, you share the excitement with your family and friends, enjoy the weekend, and when you go back to work on Monday, you are engulfed with hundreds of emails and meeting invites. You go back to your old ways and there goes all the learning to the back burner or maybe the trash can.

You have invested your time and energy in picking up valuable inputs from this book so far. You have also done some soul searching and introspection. To actually see your thoughts turn into reality, you need to have a clearly formulated strategy and implement it.

Here are some benefits you will experience by developing and implementing your personalized strategy:

- Keep you focused in making conscious progress on your objectives.

- Help you use your time and energy efficiently.

- Enable you to utilize available resources.

- Enable you to make the best use of opportunities that come your way (which you will recognize more readily as you are fully aware of what you want to accomplish).

- Give you the confidence to confront and address hurdles that you face.

- Do you need to complement these skills in some other way? How?

How do you go about creating your Strategy?

Your Strategy sets the path for your desired Purpose. This section lays out a simple and practical approach to creating your Strategy. Let us start by delving deeper into each of the aspects that should ideally be covered in your Strategy.

Step 1: The challenge/objectives:

- Accomplishing your Purpose of life, doing what you are Passionate about, leveraging your key Skills.

  Since you have already invested time and effort in identifying these aspects, you can forthrightly state them under this section. These serve as the big picture broad objectives that become the basis for you to develop an effective action plan.

Step 2: Considerations for your strategy:

- Engaging and communicating with stakeholders (those who support you as well as those who shall benefit from you):

  Bring your authentic self. Be vocal about your purpose, passion and skills, whether it is with your colleagues at your workplace or with family, friends, coach or others with a similar purpose or passion. The more you share these with people around you, the more it becomes real. There are a couple of benefits – one, people might offer to help you, second, they will keep you honest in your progress.

  Also, engage and communicate regularly with the potential beneficiaries who are the center of your purpose and passion. Share with them the value they will derive from you and how you are making progress in that direction.

- Barriers:

Identify in advance the barriers or potential pitfalls in implementing your plans. A few are listed below.

Clarity of your beneficiaries: One of the key considerations with your Passion is to have a good intersection/overlap between your passion and the demand. Do some research about your potential beneficiaries. Sometimes this could be a niche segment or it could be a new one that no one else has supported earlier. At times you may have to re-evaluate the situation and modify your plans.

Discipline and prioritization: You need to be accountable to yourself in implementing your planned actions. Your passion will help you be disciplined in dedicating time to make progress and prioritizing your activities. It is helpful to be able to *see* your Purpose when you get up each morning, motivating you to take a step in that direction every day. This will also keep you motivated towards not getting stuck in your comfort zone.

Funds/finances: Sometimes availability of funds to execute your plans can become a barrier. Be clear about the requirement of funds, the sources, when will they be required, how you will mobilise the funds. Also consider the amount of risk and uncertainty you can tolerate.

Fear of failure: It is okay to fail at doing what you are passionate about and learn from those failures. Is it not better than being great at doing something you are not passionate about?

- Resources:

  Regularly review the various resources you identified as critical to the implementation of your plans. Is it only funds/financial resources or other dependencies on certain people, equipment, infrastructure, facilities, intellectual property, technology etc.?

- Opportunities:

  Choose the opportunities largely in tune with your objectives – with your Passion and the Skills you are leveraging. Keep a tab on the changing environment. Problems that people face, their needs and their challenges keep altering. Each could be an opportunity for you to serve. At times barriers can also be converted to opportunities.

- Balancing the urgent and important:

  While some of your actions may seem 'urgent' to be implemented, keep in mind that they might be contributing to improving your current skills. Whereas, certain actions categorized as 'important' might be contributing towards longer lasting changes or transforming you. So, have a good balance of both in your action plan.

Step 3: Action plan:

- Include detailed plans for each objective to be achieved in a defined timeframe. Include description of milestones. Regularly review and track the plans and milestones. Identify any course correction required.

Integrate your actions into your normal day, what you choose to do, rather than having to chalk out a separate time to accomplish these actions.

Make your actions SMART – Specific, Measurable, Attainable, Relevant, and Time bound. A good balance of these criteria helps you stay on track, have clarity, and remain motivated to realize your objectives.

For each planned action include the what, when, how, who, how much details – Action(s) to accomplish an Objective, Support required from, Timelines to start and complete actions. Usually, the responsibility to accomplish all actions is on you.

Consider the exercises you've done earlier in this book and incorporate specific actions in your plan.

Principles: Are there any actions that you identified to better yourself on Principles? Example: Actions from the Ethics Quotient Assessment. Include them here.

Purpose: Are there any actions that you identified from the exercise – Explore your Purpose? Were you able to complete the exercise and identify your Purpose? If you did not then that is a high priority action and a pre-requisite to continue with the 'Strategy' step.

Passion: Were you able to identify the top three to five aspects that you are passionate about? If not, then that is a high priority action and a pre-requisite to continue with the Strategy step. What profession/job are you in currently, is it in tune with your passion? If not, then which profession/job is more in tune with your passion? Identify actions to move into those areas. To enable this, you may have to rebrand yourself and rewrite your resume/public profile.

Skills: Review the exercise you did to relate your Skills and Passion. Based on that, develop actions to address skill gaps. Consider these questions –

> o   What do you need to learn?
>
> o   How will you learn it?
>
> o   What experiences do you need to gain?
>
> o   How much time and expense will be involved?
>
> o   Who can support you or help you with this?
>
> o   Milestone – how will you know when you have accomplished this? (Through a certification, recognition, award etc.)

There is an important aspect to consider about skills development. *Invest more time on strengthening what you are good at rather than stressing yourself out on your weakness.*

How do you go about effectively implementing your action plan?

Strategies don't fail, their implementation does!

Implementation is where the real action takes place, "where the rubber touches the road", transforming your plans into actions. It is the most critical part of the entire process and when well executed will ensure the achievement of your objectives.

Here are a few ideas and suggestions for effectively implementing your action plan:

- It is a marathon not a sprint: Do not be tempted to rush though your action plan to change your life too fast. You need the mental stamina to maintain your pace and momentum to attain your objective.

- Act: The only way to achieve your objective is to act. Each action takes you a step closer to your Purpose. Keep your action plan or a short version of it in a place where you can see it frequently. Also use sticky notes, calendar reminders, phone reminders and other creative and practical ways of reminding you to not miss executing a planned action.

- Stay focused: Have clarity of Purpose. Be clear about why have you undertaken the action plan, why is it important for you. This will help you stay focused.

- Accountability partners: Identify people who can be honest with you about your progress on the action plan. Identify those who are interested in your transformation journey and who can help you to achieve your goals. These could be your family members, close friends, coach or mentor.

- Review regularly and plan ahead: Review the progress being made on your plan and the milestones. If you are facing hurdles then find solutions. If you have digressed then take corrective steps. Keep track of the critical components and dependencies and use them to effectively plan for the next few days or weeks. Regularly measure results.

- Stay positive: The journey you are on involves hard work. If it was easy then you would have already completed it. Do not be disheartened with minor hiccups. Enjoy the journey, learn from the experiences and stay positive.

- Be flexible: If a particular action is not helping accomplish any of your objectives, then adjust or alter your action plan. Be flexible to adopt new actions when required.

- Share your progress: Share your progress with people, even when things do not work. It will give you the opportunity to engage with them, learn their views and generate new ideas. Take them with you on your journey.

- Celebrate successes: Celebrate your successes no matter how big or small they are. This will help you keep up the momentum and your motivation. Reward yourself when you hit certain milestones. Each stride towards your objective is worth celebrating.

Strategic planning should be a regular practice and not a rare activity. Once a year is a good frequency to take into account the changing environment and to re-align yourself to your priorities. Some people do this on their birthdays and some do it at the beginning of each year. Creating your strategy is as important as implementing it.

* * * * *

In a nutshell:

 The purpose of this chapter is to help you delve deep into developing your Strategy and effectively implementing it.

"Plans are only good intentions unless they immediately degenerate into hard work." — Peter Drucker.

There is always a risk of your action plan failing but you can prevent it by driving the plan. The ultimate responsibility of its success is on you. To prevent its failure, review it, list down reasons that can contribute to its failure and incorporate mitigation measures into your action plan.

To be in your Goldilocks Zone, you need to invest time and effort in developing your Strategy and its implementation.

A key outcome for you, from this chapter, is to be able to clearly state your Purpose, your Passion and your key Skills; have visibility of considerations for your Strategy; have a SMART action plan for you to implement.

Here is a summary of how all the steps fit together in helping you get into your Goldilocks Zone.

Principles

- Actions to help you be a role model

Purpose

- Something important enough to make a positive difference in your life and that of others; love for others; and leaving a legacy behind

- Context (what you care about); Activity (that gives you the most satisfaction); Beneficiaries (for whom do you do this); Result (how do your beneficiaries transform).

Passion

- Top three to five aspects that you are passionate about – based on "what is your Purpose" and "who are you".

Skills

- Your top five skills (personality, aptitude and knowledge based)

- Relate your Skills and Passion – assess the gap and plan to address the gap

Strategy

- SMART action plan

- Implement the action plan

- Review actions and milestones

- Get the desired outcomes

Be in your **Goldilocks Zone**!

In the next and concluding chapter I have some closing thoughts to share with you.

* * * * *

Chapter 9

Conclusion and Next Steps

I would like to share my wife's journey here.

My wife was a language teacher at a school. She loved traveling and would always volunteer to lead the children's annual school excursion to various parts of the country. She also knew her city very well and would always be keen to take visiting relatives and friends around the city, showcasing unique places and experiences. Due to her knowledge of such unique places her friends would request her help to take their visiting friends or relatives around the city. She soon found herself getting busy on her weekends doing this.

One fine day she decided to convert this into her full-time occupation. She now organizes customized city tours for foreigners and tourists visiting the city through her venture called HyderabadMyWay.

That was a liberating moment for her. She is helping people experience the culture, customs and heritage of her city and she is really passionate about this.

* * *

In this last chapter I am going to tie everything together for you and help you take the next steps.

- The five steps to be in your Goldilocks Zone

- You control the legacy you want to leave

- Eudemonia

- Plan A+

- Epilogue

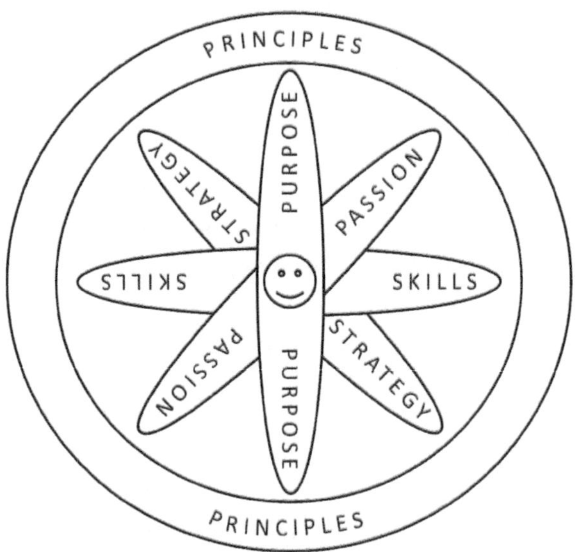

The five steps to be in your Goldilocks Zone

You have now read through the five steps to be in your Goldilocks Zone. You have also completed the exercises to help gain clarity on each of them from your own perspective.

In a nutshell: With a purpose to serve others selflessly, you do what you are passionate about, leveraging your skills/ capabilities and resources, always following the path of being ethical.

By now you should be able to complete this key sentence for yourself:

My purpose of life is to ___________________________________
_______________________________________by doing (what
I'm passionate about) _____________________________________

____

____
_____________by leveraging my skills in __________________

____

____
________________________________and imbibing ethical behavior.

You control the legacy you want to leave:

Imagine you meet some people who are on their death bed and they tell you how they wish they could change how they lived their life:

- "I earned a lot of money but at this stage of my life I don't have the satisfaction of having accomplished something meaningful."

- "I wish I had pursued what I enjoyed doing rather than getting driven by the salary hikes and incentives to do what I didn't enjoy."

- "I have spent my life buying comforts for myself and my family. I don't think I could buy happiness."

- "I wish I could tell my parents (family/boss) what I wanted to do in life rather than doing what made them happy."

Or, would you rather hear people leaving a legacy like the following?

- "I did what mattered to me the most, passionately supporting the community for causes that were important to me."

- "I transformed my life from the bad conditions that I was born in, to taking full responsibility for the changes I wanted to see in my life and contributing positively to others in a similar situation."

- "I was privileged to have been born with a silver spoon. I am happy that I could utilize the resources I had in improving the living conditions of those who were less fortunate."

- "I have faced many ups and downs in life like many others. But I am happy that I was able to make a difference in the lives of hundreds of people by sharing my experience with them and helping them learn from my experiences."

Does that help you leverage your purpose to lead yourself into a satisfying life? Does this help you think about what you want to be remembered for?

Some people may argue that they are regular people who just leave what they earned for their children and their children are their legacy.

Leaving a legacy of your choice is in your control. You can use the power of your life for the good of those you connect with, from your families, friends, colleagues, to your communities.

Knowing what legacy you want to leave serves you like a compass to steer you with purpose even when you are hesitant about something.

Eudemonia:

While reading about the views various people have shared on their purpose of life, I came across several words and phrases like – happiness, satisfaction, self-actualization, fulfillment, etc. I came across a word that was new to me, eudemonia.

Happiness is a temporary moment, while satisfaction is a longer lasting feeling that tends to build up over time, based on realizing your objectives and leading the kind of life you wanted.

Eudemonia or 'eudaimonia' is more constant, common and realistic in our daily lives. Eudemonia implies a positive and divine state of being that humanity is able to strive toward and possibly reach. Eudaimonia could be translated as: fulfillment, living a good (moral) life, human flourishing, and moral or spiritual success.

Models of eudaimonia in psychology and positive psychology emerged from early work on self-actualization and the means of its accomplishment by researchers such as Abraham Maslow.

Plan A+:

After his bachelors' degree, Randheer acquired a diploma in sales. He was always passionate about animal rights and wildlife photography but his parents strongly felt that he would not be able to make a career pursuing that field. He was involved in selling computer hardware for several years and had built a successful career in the field. He felt insecure about transitioning into wildlife photography as he did not want a break in his career (read 'regular income'). On weekends he used to attend wildlife photography camps and post beautiful photographs on social media. One day he was approached by a wildlife photographic equipment company with an offer to join them as a regional sales head. This was a perfect fit for him. He was close to his purpose and passion and had the right skills. Making that move was the most exciting phase for him.

Many of my classmates, friends and colleagues are employed or working on aspects that are hardly related to their college degrees.

This is actually good.

As a young kid Sanjana had seen her elder brother go through depression after not qualifying for a seat in one of the IITs (a common dream among Indian children and their parents). She was keen to support children and as a bright student herself did her engineering and started coaching classes for XI and XII grade students. Apart from conducting classes, she devoted a lot of her time in providing career guidance to students. Seeing her passion in guiding children, one of the parents who was a psychologist, suggested that Sanjana take up a professional course in psychology or coaching. Sanjana did that. She invested in doing a course in child psychology and on completion took up student counseling as a full-time profession. That was exactly what she wanted to do in her life. It resonated with her purpose and passion, and she had the right skills for it.

People usually have a plan B if something does not go well. I would call this an A+ plan as it can turn out to be better than the original plan.

If you look around you will find many more examples of how people discovered over a period of time what they really wanted to do in life and started moving in that direction. It is never too late! The key is to proactively ask yourself this question, probe the answers, plan your roadmap, and take action!

Epilogue:

According to my research, while people rated 4.6 on a 7-point scale for the statement "I have invested time and energy in developing a strategy to accomplish my life's purpose", only 4.2 on 7 "have been able to successfully implement their strategy to accomplish their life's purpose".

Dear Reader, the next step really is to take action. You have the framework; you have invested your time and energy in understanding yourself better, you have invested in developing a plan, it is now time to implement your plan – ACT!

In this journey, if you need someone to support you then feel free to reach out to me. You can interact with me and also leverage content that you may find relevant, on my website – www.rohitrchowdhry.com

As you might recollect, my purpose is to engage with people to support them to explore their full potential in living a satisfying life. What is yours?

You have now seen all the steps involved in helping you get into your Goldilocks Zone. This is by discovering and understanding the PURPOSE of your life better, knowing what your PASSION is, and actually doing it, and leveraging your key SKILLS. You are doing all this by developing and implementing a STRATEGY, while abiding by PRINCIPLES – moving towards the maximum standards (of ethics), and creating a role model behavior.

Your Goldilocks Zone is where you consciously take steps to contribute to selflessly serve others in your own unique way, doing something you are passionate about, leveraging your skills and abilities. When all these factors work in harmony, then you are completely in your Goldilocks Zone. Your Goldilocks Zone is the perfect combination of conditions where **you can make the best of your life**.

Best wishes for you to get into **your** Goldilocks Zone!

* * * * *

Chapter 10

Overview of the Survey

I ran an online survey in 2020 that had 565 respondents.

Name of the survey: Making the best of life

Respondent profile:

- Gender:
  - o Female: 232
  - o Male: 327
  - o Other: 6
- Highest education:
  - o Bachelors: 172
  - o Masters: 359
  - o Others: 34 (mostly PhD, MPhil, others)
- Age group (years):
  - o 18–25: 38
  - o 26–35: 80
  - o 36–45: 196
  - o 46–55: 204

- o   56–65: 40

- o   66+: 7

- Occupation:

  - o   Employed: 362

  - o   Self-employed: 122

  - o   Unemployed: 13

  - o   Student: 24

  - o   Retired: 19

  - o   Homemaker: 25

- Personality:

  - o   Introvert: 251; Extrovert: 314

  - o   Goal oriented: 171; Relationship oriented: 394

In summary, the respondents included those who had at least completed their Graduation, a good gender mix, spread across age-groups, a mix of occupations, and a combination of personality styles. Most of the respondents were in the age group of 36–55 (71%).

Survey themes: Largely rating-based questions and multiple-choice questions covered these themes –

- Satisfaction with life

- Importance of ethics

- Passion

- Skills required to do what one is passionate about

- Strategy to accomplish one's life's purpose

- Legacy one wants to leave

- Purpose of life

- Zeal to make life meaningful

- Need for a mentor or guide to learn how to be truly satisfied in life.

* * * * *

About the Author

Rohit R Chowdhry is a Life Coach, Executive Coach, and a Career Transition Coach, certified by the International Coaching Federation. He has over three decades of work experience in MNCs, playing strategic leadership roles and working with global clients. He has coached and mentored several management level professionals and understands the hurdles people face in being successful with their careers and achieving satisfaction in their life.

He engages with people to support them in exploring their full potential, to live a satisfying life. He also leverages his experience in providing strategic and operational guidance and leadership for off-shoring of shared services.

His hobbies include drawing, painting, photography, traveling, reading and listening to music.

You can connect with him on his website www.rohitrchowdhry. com where his other social media links are also provided. Scan the QR code to go to his website: